WHAT'S
YOUR
FUTURE
WORTH?

WHAT'S YOUR FUTURE WORTH?

USING PRESENT VALUE TO MAKE BETTER DECISIONS

Peter Neuwirth, FSA

Berrett–Koehler Publishers, Inc.
a BK Life book

Berrett-Koehler Publishers, Inc.
1333 Broadway, Suite 1000
Oakland, CA 94612-1921
Tel: (510) 817-2277   Fax: (510) 817-2278   www.bkconnection.com

Ordering Information
Quantity sales. Special discounts are available on quantity purchases by corporations, associations, and others. For details, contact the "Special Sales Department" at the Berrett-Koehler address above.
Individual sales. Berrett-Koehler publications are available through most bookstores. They can also be ordered directly from Berrett-Koehler: Tel: (800) 929-2929; Fax: (802) 864-7626; www.bkconnection.com
Orders for college textbook/course adoption use. Please contact Berrett-Koehler: Tel: (800) 929-2929; Fax: (802) 864-7626.
Orders by U.S. trade bookstores and wholesalers. Please contact Ingram Publisher Services, Tel: (800) 509-4887; Fax: (800) 838-1149; E-mail: customer.service@ingrampublisherservices.com; or visit www.ingrampublisherservices.com/Ordering for details about electronic ordering.

Berrett-Koehler and the BK logo are registered trademarks of Berrett-Koehler Publishers, Inc.

Printed in the United States of America

Berrett-Koehler books are printed on long-lasting acid-free paper. When it is available, we choose paper that has been manufactured by environmentally responsible processes. These may include using trees grown in sustainable forests, incorporating recycled paper, minimizing chlorine in bleaching, or recycling the energy produced at the paper mill.

Library of Congress Cataloging-in-Publication Data

Neuwirth, Peter.
What's your future worth? : using present value to make better decisions / by Peter Neuwirth, FSA.
     pages cm
Includes bibliographical references.
ISBN 978-1-62656-301-8 (pbk.)
1. Investments–Decision making. 2. Finance–Decision making. 3. Present value analysis. 4. Valuation. I. Title.
HG4515.N467 2014
332.024–dc23
                              2014041508

First Edition
20 19 18 17 16 15   10 9 8 7 6 5 4 3 2 1

Cover Design: Ian Koviak/The Book Designers

Dedicated to the memory of
Robert Frohlich, 1955–2010
Who taught us all that
nothing *is impossible to imagine*

Contents

Preface

When I was a teenager, my father—a mathematician who spent most of his career working as a cryptologist for the US government—gave me a little book written by G. H. Hardy called *A Mathematician's Apology*. He said he wanted me to understand the way he thought about the world. At that age, I wasn't very interested in my father's world, particularly as he and it seemed distinctly out of step with what seemed to be happening all around us. It was the early 1970s, times were changing fast, and the musings of an old British math professor did not seem at all relevant to my life. The book stayed unread for a long time, but one day in my junior year at college, having only recently enrolled in my first math class in years (despite having gone all the way through calculus while in high school), something made me pick it up and start reading. I guess part of it may have been a growing feeling that as much as I wanted to deny it, math was in my blood and it was high time I came to grips with and understood what it meant to "think like a mathematician." The message I got from the book, and later from my father when we talked, was that one doesn't choose to be a mathematician; rather, one is compelled to become one. My father said it was like having "a monkey on my back" and confessed that most of the time he simply couldn't help himself thinking about mathematics or seeing the world in mathematical terms. It was something he never wished for me.

It turns out that I didn't become a mathematician but instead became an actuary. Being an actuary is certainly not as obsessive or all-consuming as being a theoretical mathematician, and as actuaries we tend to be somewhat more comfortable with normal human interaction. However, being an actuary does mean looking at the world in a unique way, particularly when it comes to three elements of life that we all have to deal with—time, risk, and money. As actuaries, we are trained to balance these three elements to help manage many of the financial security programs that—though central to our lives— most of us don't think about too often, such as insurance, pensions, Social Security, and so forth. Important as this is, I believe that the actuarial perspective can have even broader application. For many years, I've been thinking about just what that means and how to communicate it to others.

This book is a result of that thinking and is my attempt to put into words the actuarial perspective, to share the insights that my thirty-five years as an actuary have given me on not just how to make financial decisions, but how to think about and make many other important choices that arise in life. This book will not teach you how to be an actuary—it won't even teach you how to think like an actuary—but it will give you an important tool that you can use in your own life to make better decisions.

That tool is called Present Value and even though it has a mathematical definition, you don't need any math to use it. Fundamentally, Present Value is a way to think about all the ways the future may unfold and boil down those possibilities to an "apples to apples" choice that can be made today. It is a framework and a process that you can use to make all kinds of decisions ranging from the mundane (e.g., whether to buy a new car or how much to contribute to your 401(k)) to the most important (e.g., when to change careers or how to make life-and-death medical decisions).

So who is this book for? Since I believe that everyone who has to make life decisions can benefit from thinking more systematically about the choices they face, in a sense, this book is for everyone, or at least everyone who wants to get better at making decisions.

The above notwithstanding, there are certain people for whom this book will be particularly valuable. For example, I think that those who advise others on financial, medical, and lifestyle choices may find learning about the actuarial perspective and Present Value very useful indeed.

Finally, because I am an actuary who will be talking honestly and directly about the profession, I expect that many, if not most, actuaries and those considering actuarial work as a profession will be interested in hearing what I have to say.

Throughout this book, I will talk about how I've used the actuarial perspective and Present Value to make choices in my life. I've tried to distill that process down to a set of principles and steps that you can take with you to think more systematically and clearly about your future and how it will be shaped by the choices you make.

While it's not a formula or recipe to live a better life, those principles and that systematic approach to decision making has allowed me to make decisions with more awareness and a clearer understanding of the future consequences of my choices, and I truly hope it does for you as well.

Introduction

THINKING ABOUT THE FUTURE IN A SYSTEMATIC WAY

It has become a cliché to say that we live in an "Information Age," but the fact of the matter is that the amount of data available to us has exploded and grown almost beyond our ability to comprehend. At the same time, we as individuals are, more than ever, inundated with choices in our daily lives, and unlike the past, these choices now come associated with an overwhelming amount of information. Some of that information we seek and some is thrust upon us, but in total, rather than help us, the data often simply paralyzes us. From the mundane consumer choices we make every day to life-and-death medical decisions, we are given facts, figures, and recommendations but no *systematic* way to sort through that information and actually decide.

In almost all cases where we have an important choice, we are asked to make a decision in the present that will have consequences sometime in the future. This book is intended to show you a straightforward and systematic way to make those choices without getting lost or confused by too much information. The key tool we will use is called *Present Value,* and it is one that actuaries have used for over a century to do their job.

Despite any impression you may have (given by actuaries or others) that Present Value is a complicated or technical concept of only limited applicability, the idea is straightforward and can be useful for anyone—at least anyone who has ever had to make a choice between *now* and *later,* anyone who has ever had to decide whether or not to quit their awful job and follow their bliss, whether to buy that new car or increase their 401(k) contributions, whether to get married, when to have kids, and on and on.

How People Choose

Typically, people make decisions from one of several perspectives. First, they might make decisions based on the past, focusing on what has worked before or how the decision at hand is similar to one previously addressed. These people make their decisions based on experience.

Second, they might, as Eckhart Tolle in *The Power of Now*[1] suggests, focus on what they see in the "here and now," adhering to Tolle's philosophy that the future "doesn't really exist." Such people feel that they should just be in the present moment, trusting the "power of now" to guide them. Somewhat related to this group are the people who base their choices on their faith or intuition, trusting that some unseen force (or perhaps their own "intention" or "aspirations") will guide them to the right decision. These people make their decisions "from their gut."

Finally, many (perhaps most) people—including those who tend to use the first two approaches—do try to think about the future in a logical way and consider the immediate and long-term consequences of the choices they face, deciding on a course of action based on intellectual analysis and a projection of future events. However, such people usually try and figure out what they think will happen and then act accordingly. In the best of circumstances, they might consider a couple of different scenarios. But even here, the decision maker will most often come to a conclusion as to what is most likely to occur and then make their choice on that basis.

In fact, there seems to be—at least for this third group—an almost universal feeling that trying to figure out what is *actually going to happen* is basically the only way to think about the future. There is a better way. For reasons that we will discuss shortly, I would propose that we will *never* know for sure what the future holds and that we need a different attitude toward what will happen and what we should do now to prepare for it.

A New Way to Decide

In the next few chapters, I will talk about a very powerful tool called "Present Value" that everyone can use to make better decisions. In a nutshell, Present Value is the concept that allows you to think about the future and the present at the same time, to put them on an equal footing, to make "apples to apples" comparisons.

Most of us live in both the future and the present. Some focus more on one than the other (I ignore for now those who live in the past), but almost all of us do so sequentially. The neuroscientists out there may say that that is because it's physically impossible to be in both places simultaneously, but be that as it may, I would argue that by using Present Value you can come as close as possible to keeping the balance between the two front and center.

What do I mean when I say we should consider the present and the future at the same time? How does one do that and why is it useful? In this book we will look at many of the choices that face us as individuals or collectively and see how a different way of looking at these questions can lead to better decisions and arguably a better society as a whole.

We will call this approach "the actuarial perspective" because it is actuaries who most often use Present Value and it is they who originally adopted the approach I describe. The difference is that while actuaries generally use Present Value in a very narrow and limited way, the fact of the matter is that anyone can use Present Value in their own life and apply it to all kinds of decisions that actuaries would never think of using it for. While Present Value as actuaries use it has a technical and mathematical definition, you don't need math to understand it and use it in your own life.

At its core, Present Value simply means the value *today* of something that *may* happen *tomorrow*. Every day we are faced with choices, and those choices all have consequences that (generally) only manifest themselves sometime in the future. Most critically, the decisions we make when we choose between two different alternatives lead to *different futures.* Imagining what those different futures might look like is a critical step in making the right choice.

So far I haven't said anything new. Almost all of us imagine the future impact of the choices we make, but what distinguishes the actuarial perspective from the way people normally make decisions is that by using Present Value we can think about our choices in a *systematic* way that takes into account some aspects of the future that we rarely consider. In particular, when we use Present Value we try to imagine not just what we think the future impact of our choices will be, but rather consider all the possible futures each choice might lead to. And even more important than considering all the future consequences that a given choice might lead to, we consider *when* those future consequences might show themselves.

In summary, using the actuarial perspective means *thinking about the future in a systematic way and using the idea of Present Value—the value today of something that might happen in the future—to make better choices.*

In the rest of this book, I will explain in more detail what Present Value is. I will also show you how to use it and think systematically about the choices we all face every day. By the end of the book, you won't be an actuary, and you won't have a formula to apply to every decision you face, but you will be able to think more systematically and use a different process to making important decisions.

To get started, let's look at a mundane example where the actuarial perspective allowed me to make a

better choice than I could have if I had not known about
Present Value.

The Perfect Running Shoe

For most of my adult life I was a jogger, and like most
runners, I was very particular about the shoes I wear.
From the moment I began running regularly, the
"Saucony Jazz" was my favorite shoe. It was incredibly
comfortable and "cushiony." To get this effect, the
sole contained a special kind of foam that molded to
my foot and absorbed the shocks of the road better
than any other shoe on the market. To my knowledge,
Saucony was the only company that used this particular
foam. About twenty years ago, the company decided to
discontinue the "Jazz" as well as the use of its special
foam (apparently most runners did not like the fact that
after several months the foam compressed and lost some
of its cushioning effect). So what does this have to do
with Present Value? Well, after the announcement, all
Saucony Jazz shoes were put on sale for 50% off and I
was faced with a difficult choice—specifically how many
pairs to buy. This was my favorite shoe, and after the
existing stock was sold, I would *never* be able to purchase
one again. On the other hand, I could only use one pair
at a time so if I decided to buy, let's say, twenty pairs at
a cost of $50 per pair, I would be paying $1000 today
for something that, under the best of circumstances,
I wouldn't be using for several years. But it was more
complicated than that. I had to consider the fact that
I might not get a chance to use some of those shoes.
I might, either by choice or because of injury, stop

running. I had to consider the space I would need to store the shoes and the hassle of packing, storing, and moving them if necessary. I also had to consider whether there would be some new technological development in shoes that would produce something even better than the Jazz.

Finally, I had to consider the economics. $50 per pair was a pretty good price. But how good? Would prices on shoes rise like the price of gas or would they fall like the price of personal computers? And if I didn't buy the shoes, what would I do with the $1000 I didn't spend? Would I invest it? If so, how much could I expect to earn and at what risk? My point is not that there is a clear way to incorporate all these factors into a calculation. In fact, I doubt that a formal Present Value calculation would be of any practical use in this case. My point instead is to show that when we make even a mundane decision like buying running shoes it is helpful to use the concept of Present Value to make our choice.

So how did I approach the problem? In brief, I used the actuarial perspective to make my decision.

Even though actuaries use a lot of math in their calculations, using the actuarial perspective in the real world requires virtually no math whatsoever. Instead, all it requires is a systematic approach and the use of the core concept of Present Value to equate the value of things that happen at various times in the future to the value of things today. Here—and in many future examples—I used the following 5-step process to develop and compare Present Values to make my decision:

1. Define the choices to be made.

2. Imagine all (or as many as you can) of the possible

futures that might arise from each choice, focusing not just on what could happen, but on when it could happen as well.

3. Evaluate, to the extent possible, the relative likelihood of each possible future.

4. Introspect deeply and in a detailed way to consider how much more value should be placed on things that will happen in the near future vs. things that will happen in the distant future.

5. Sum up the values of the consequences of each choice (i.e., determine the Present Value of each alternative).

The only "calculation" involved in the process above is in step 5, and even here, many cases will require nothing more than adding and comparing. The really hard part of the process—and the part that most actuaries spend years learning how to do well— is in steps 2–4. We will talk at much greater length about each of these steps, including the attitudes and state of mind required to perform them well, but as my running shoe purchase illustrates, the tasks themselves are pretty straightforward.

Step 1 seems obvious, but even here, before thinking about a decision, it is important to make sure that we have identified exactly what our alternatives are. In this case, when I thought about how many running shoes to buy, I only thought about visiting my local running shoe stores and the inventory that they had on hand. I did not consider traveling around the country or contacting Saucony directly, which could have allowed me to buy 100 pairs of shoes instead of the thirty or fewer that I considered. Part of that was because I wasn't willing to go through the *immediate* effort of expanding the amount of shoes I could consider buying and part of it was that I knew that no matter what, I would almost certainly never be able to use all 100 pairs even if I kept running for the rest of my life.

Step 2 is perhaps the most important part of the process and the one where, in my view, most people do not take the time to do well. Imagining *all* the possible consequences of a given action is impossible, but most of us attach ourselves quite quickly to one or two possibilities that we think are most likely or seem most obvious and then don't think too much about any other factors. The range of possible futures is *vast*—in some ways that is what makes life interesting—and spending a little extra time considering more than just what you *think* is going to happen is key to evaluating the impact of what *might* happen. Everyone has their own way of doing this, but for me it is important to adopt an attitude of quiet, non-attachment, and curiosity as I try to imagine all that might ensue. I spent a fair amount of time on this step before I headed out to the local shopping mall. I imagined what the future might look like with only a couple of pairs of Sauconys to run in versus what I would experience with a closet full of the boxes waiting to be opened many years in the future. I tried to think about when I would be using those shoes and just how much value I would get out of them, taking into account possible injuries, the initial and ongoing cost of shoes, available alternatives, future improvements in shoe technology, and so forth, as well as the ongoing "costs" I would experience throughout those futures, such as storage, moving, and foregone investments.

On its surface, step 3 can be intimidating, but it is often simpler than it appears. After we have imagined the possibilities, it is important to consider the relative likelihood of each, but it is rarely necessary to assign actual probabilities to different scenarios. Instead, using intuition and common sense goes a long way. Here, for example, I didn't do an explicit calculation of the probabilities associated with all the unknowns (e.g., how long my running career would last), but I did consider in a general sort of way the likelihood of various scenarios and factored my own intuition about where things were going into my determination. In some aspects I was right (e.g., I thought it likely that shoe prices would go up but investment returns—at least mine—would be low), in some I was wrong (I thought there would be a better than fifty-fifty chance I'd have to stop running within ten years but in fact didn't get injured and have to stop running until I was in my mid-fifties), and in others I was somewhere in between (eventually, as I expected, shoe technology caught up with Saucony, but it took longer than I thought it would). When step 3 was complete and I had considered the relative likelihood of each future scenario, it seemed that I would need about fifteen to twenty pairs of shoes to last until my running career ended or shoe technology improved, but that is not how many I bought. The reason was step 4.

Step 4 is the one part of the process that is truly unique to the actuarial perspective, and we will spend quite some time on this one. In my experience (validated by scholars like Daniel Kahneman, who wrote *Thinking, Fast and Slow,* as well as many other researchers who have performed similar studies[2]), people generally do not think about the relative importance of similar events that happen at *different* points in the future, and when faced with choices highlighting this difference (e.g., "would you like to have $100 today, $150 a year from now, or $1000 ten years from now?"), their answers are inconsistent and respondents cannot explain their rationale.[3] As you read through the book, I will be encouraging you to think hard about how you personally value benefits that you receive immediately vs. benefits that you will have to wait a modest amount of time for (e.g., a few months) vs. other benefits that will take years to come your way. By thinking clearly about this aspect of the choices we face, we can apply some rigor and rationality to how we evaluate *now* the choices we make today but whose effects will only be felt in the future. The technical term for what we will be doing here is to develop a "discount rate" that will allow us to work our way from the future back to the present and create the "apples to apples" comparisons that we need to make informed choices.

In the end, I bought four pairs of shoes, and while that was fewer than the number that would have lasted until New Balance came out with a running shoe every bit as good as the Jazz, when one considers step 4, it was still a good decision and a far better one than what I would have come up with had I simply got attached to a particular future. In my case, part of the reason that I only bought four pairs of shoes instead of the fifteen to twenty that I would have needed to last until the New Balance shoes were developed was that I valued the ability to run comfortably in the very near term (as well as the money I would save by not buying the extra pairs) far more than I valued my running experience five or ten years in the future. Essentially, I applied a very *high* discount rate to my future experience in order to compare it to the cost of buying the shoes in the present. In chapter 4, you will find a more detailed explanation of how a discount rate works, but for now just think of it as the opposite of an interest rate. An interest rate makes money grow from the present into the future, while a discount rate takes money in the future and shrinks it back to its value today.

One secret I will share with you is that as much as some in the actuarial profession may say otherwise, the fact of the matter is that, for any particular question, there really is no "right" discount rate to use, particularly when it comes to a decision that is individual in nature. Choosing the right discount rate is vitally important, but no one can choose it for you, it is too dependent on *your* particular circumstances and the nature of the decision to be made. That being said, my hope is that with the insights provided by generations of actuaries who have considered the problem deeply and the information and observations that follow, you will be equipped to make that determination for yourself.

Finally, there is step 5, "doing the calculation." Again, this is a part of the Present Value determination that in some ways is the *least* important part of the process. There are certainly situations where such calculations are important and complicated to make. If there weren't, we actuaries would not be paid as much as we are. However, in most real-life situations, if steps 1–4 have been done in a systematic and thorough manner, the answer will often be obvious. The important point to remember here is that we are usually not trying to determine a specific number—we are simply trying to make a decision and most times it is simply a question of which Present Value is *greater,* rather than what exactly the Present Value *is.* This was very much the case as I was thinking about my shoe purchase. In particular, I wasn't trying to determine a precise number of shoes to buy—I was simply trying to decide whether to buy none, a couple, a few, or more than a few pairs and which of those choices represented the greatest Present Value to me. There was no magic to the number four. In fact, if I remember right, four was the number of shoes in stock at the first store I went to, and given that I knew I didn't want to buy that many additional pairs, I decided that it wasn't worth travelling across town to look for more. That is the way Present Value works in the real world.

If it were only relatively minor decisions around clearance sales and running shoes that called for Present Value considerations, that would be one thing. But in my view, where using Present Value becomes vitally important is when we are faced with the really important decisions in our lives, the forks in the road where the path we choose can lead to vastly different futures.

In the rest of this book, we will explore many different kinds of decisions and how Present Value can and should be factored into making them. We will also discuss in a deeper way the nature of the elements that go into present value—the *present* (where we live and when we have to choose), the *future* (when the impact of our choices will emerge), *time* (the bridge that connects the two), *risk* (the way we distinguish between possible futures), and *money* (the shortcut metric we often use to measure "value"). Most important, however, we will talk about *how* to use Present Value, what attitudes and approaches are central to actuaries' (or at least this actuary's) approach when they think about the future, and the process they go through to choose or recommend choices to be made by others.

Chapter 1

MORDECAI'S PROPOSITION— A QUESTION OF PRESENT VALUE

"If I gave you $10,000 today would you be willing to give me 1% of all your future paychecks?"

Mordecai Schwartz, FSA,
to a young actuarial student

It was 1979 and I had just started my first job out of college as an actuarial student with Connecticut General Life Insurance in Hartford, Connecticut. My boss was a long-haired libertarian from Arkansas who spoke so quietly you had to lean in close to hear him. He was edgy, sarcastic, and rebellious (he had only recently caved in to the company's insistent demand that he get a haircut and begin wearing decent clothes to work), but he was also one of the top actuaries in the company with a nose for risk and a wizard-like ability to make the numbers sing and dance. He always said that what makes a good actuary is not his or her ability to calculate, or even to use sophisticated mathematical techniques to evaluate risk, but rather to understand the music in the numbers—to hear the melody, to anticipate the chord changes, and most importantly to detect the false note. He said that a good actuary should be able to look at two columns of numbers with vague headings like "prior year actual" or "current year allocated" and, with no knowledge of what the figures were supposed to represent, be able to immediately identify the wrong number.

But before I could even begin to develop those skills, I first had to learn and internalize the concept that is at the heart of all actuarial work—specifically the notion of Present Value. I was, of course, given books and files to read to learn the math behind Present Value,[4] but Mordecai also wanted to find a way to teach me the practical importance of understanding how Present Value works, and true to his nature, he found a way to permanently embed that concept while at the same time benefiting himself and having some fun, at my expense.

You see, Mordecai was a gambler and game player. An excellent chess player, he was even better at poker, where he could combine his expertise in strategy, psychology, and probability with his fiercely competitive nature to outsmart his colleagues and make a little extra cash. He also enjoyed creating propositions and making bets— from politics to sports, from financial market behavior to actuarial matters, he was always willing to "put his money where his mouth was." For him, it was often less about the money and more about the elegance and virtues of the proposition itself.

Not surprisingly, most of his bets involved Present Value calculations, at least in an indirect way, and the first one he proposed to me had it at its core. Having just passed the first three (out of ten) actuarial exams with only a minimum of effort, I opined one day that all the talk I'd heard about how long, hard, and treacherous the path was to becoming a Licensed Actuary[5] was obviously nonsense and that I expected to be able to move through the rest of the exams without any difficulty. Mordecai smiled slyly and asked if I was willing to bet $500 that I would pass all of the final seven exams on my first try. Being overconfident and not understanding either risk *or* Present Value, I readily agreed. Of course this was an incredibly stupid move on my part. First, I had no idea what the next seven exams were like (Mordecai did). Second, even if my chances of passing any given exam on the first try was 90%, the probability of passing all seven without a miss was less than 50% (0.9 raised to the 7th power is about 0.48). Most importantly, I completely missed the fact that if I failed an exam, I could lose the bet years sooner than if I passed all the exams the first time. In other words, even if I won the bet, I wouldn't collect for at least another four years (exams were given every 6 months) but if I lost I would have to pay Mordecai as soon as I failed, and this could happen as soon as the next exam. Given that interest rates at that time were well over 10%, this factor alone should have caused me to ask for odds.

So the fourth exam came a few months later and I completely bombed it. I walked out of the room knowing absolutely that I had failed. In a panic about the $500 that I didn't have but would shortly owe my boss, I considered my options. The only factor that I realized was in my favor was that I knew I had failed but Mordecai did not (results would not be available for another two months) and so I had two months to negotiate a settlement. Eventually, I agreed to pay $50 immediately to extricate myself from the bet. Now to this day I wonder why Mordecai agreed. Perhaps he bought my presentation (I expressed supreme confidence that I'd passed but realized how long I would have to wait for my payoff and how I had underestimated future risks), perhaps he was being kind and/or didn't want to risk the non-financial fallout when it became known how he'd taken advantage of his naïve young student. Or maybe he was just very risk averse, and having done *his own* Present Value calculation, decided that $50 was a reasonable estimate of the current worth of the future outcome of the bet. No matter what, it was a lesson well learned and one for which I owe Mordecai a debt far greater than the $50 price.

But Mordecai was not done. He had one more lesson about Present Value that he wanted to teach me, and this was the one that more than any set me on the path that has led to this book.

Mordecai's Proposition

Shortly before the end of my time working for him, Mordecai came to me with an intriguing proposition. He asked me whether I would be willing to "sell" him a piece of my future earnings. Specifically he offered me $10,000 to enter into a contract with him whereby at the end of each year I would give him 1% of what I'd earned during the prior twelve months. At the time I was making less than $20,000 and so for the current year the bill would be under $200 and even for the next few years it seemed that I would only have to pay him a few hundred dollars. The idea of receiving fifty times the initial amount in one lump sum certainly seemed appealing, but having only just narrowly escaped a financial disaster, I decided this time to consider the question more carefully before I gave him an answer.

For the first time in my life, I tried to think systematically about the future and what it was worth to me in the present. I had to imagine what the rest of my earning career would look like. I had to consider *all* the possibilities—not only what my career trajectory might look like (e.g., would I rise to some senior actuarial position, change careers and strike it rich, or crash and burn struggling to get by), but also what the future economic world would be like. Would the market for actuaries get better or worse? Would inflation increase, rendering 1% of my future earnings so large as to make the $10,000 I got seem like a pittance? What would I do with the $10,000? If I invested it, what kind of return could I expect to receive and would it offset any inflation that might raise the annual amount I had to pay each year? These were the measurable factors, but there was far more to the proposition that had to be considered.

I needed to think about what it would mean to me to have this additional "tax" burdening me for the rest of my life. One thing I realized was that if I made a lot of money, the bill would be big but I could afford it. On the other hand, if times were tough, I would struggle to make even a modest payment. And then there were the relationships to consider. How would any future wife or family feel about this added "baggage"? And what about my relationship with Mordecai himself? He and I had a decent enough relationship, but what would it mean to be "in business" with him for the next few decades? Assuming my future working career would be at least forty years, lurking in the back of my mind was also another aspect of the proposition that suggested I should grab the money. Specifically, it seemed to me that while the $10,000 was a sure thing, would I really have to pay Mordecai each and every year for the next forty? Wasn't it possible that some radical change in either his or my circumstance would render the contract unenforceable or moot? The $10,000 could be spent immediately, but were those future payments equally real? And finally, I had to grapple with the most important question in any Present Value calculation—what relative value should I put on amounts payable ten, twenty, or forty years in the future compared to the weight I put on amounts today. I had to figure out, for the first time, what my personal rate of discount was and—interestingly—whether it was different when I considered the value of the next few years' payments compared to the payments I would be making in the very distant future.

In the end, I made the right decision and turned him down. I won't go through how each of the five steps played out, but for me, step 4 turned out to be the critical one. The $10,000 just wasn't as valuable to me as the large payments I expected to make down the road, and the freedom from such a long-term future obligation was too important for me to give up. For this particular decision, I used a relatively *low* personal rate of discount though others facing the same choice whose discount rate is higher might have done the right thing by accepting the money.

But whether or not I made the right decision is not the point. What is important is that Mordecai's proposition is the essential question of this book. Namely, what is *your* future worth, and how do you determine it? For almost forty years I've been thinking about this question, and in the next few chapters I will tell you what I've discovered about how to answer it.

Chapter 2

PRESENT VALUE IN THE DAY-TO-DAY WORLD

The idea of Present Value lurks just below the surface of an overwhelming number of decisions we make on a day-to-day basis, and being aware of its presence and how to incorporate it will lead to making better choices. In this chapter, we will look at a few of the common types of mundane decisions that arise in everyday life and see how taking a few extra minutes to think in terms of Present Value can often shed an entirely new light on those questions.

Do We Need a New Refrigerator?

Shortly after I began writing this book, my wife came to me and said that she was pretty sure we needed a new refrigerator. Needless to say, this was not exactly welcome news, and my fiscal defenses were immediately mobilized. My first response—perhaps familiar to many of you—was, "Why? The one we have is still working fine. And besides, it's only seven years old, and the guy at Sears told us it should last ten or fifteen years at least." I had a sinking feeling that this was the first volley in a campaign designed to achieve a comprehensive kitchen remodeling. But my wife knows me better than to lead with esthetics, and so she quite reasonably pointed out that while it was true that the fridge was still keeping everything cool, the outside of it seemed to be running hotter than normal and as our electric bill had recently been outrageously high she was sure we would actually *save* money if we bought a new one. If true, this was a powerful argument and one that I could not effectively parry. Essentially, she was saying that putting all the nonquantifiable reasons aside (and believe me she was loaded for bear if I ever engaged in *that* discussion) the *Present Value* of our future refrigeration expenses would be less if we purchased a new one now than if we waited for the old one to live out its life using up more and more electricity to do so. Clearly, the question called for just the kind of systematic thinking described earlier, so let's see how I applied our 5-step process.

Step 1—clarify the choice. While the decision to be made was clear (to buy or not), the cost of each option was not. So first I had to figure out how much more in electricity we were now spending than we would if we bought a new refrigerator. The cost of the electricity on the new models was easy to determine, as such figures were prominently displayed (in some cases more prominently than the price tag) on the front door of each model in the showroom. The tricky part was figuring out how much the current one was costing us. One way to approach this was to assume that before it "broke," our refrigerator electric costs were the same as those on the new model and that what we would save would be the amount by which our electric bill had gone up since the current one started running hot. But even with this simpler calculation, there were two problems. The first was purely psychological—I just didn't want to believe that we had a problem, that things had changed, and that the original projections given to us by the salesman at the store where we purchased the refrigerator were simply not valid any more. The second one was all the "noise" in the calculation—such as all the month-to-month variations in weather, vacations, light use, and so forth (not to mention price changes)—that affect the bill. Both of these issues come up again and again whenever one tries to apply Present Value to real-world decisions.

I will spare you the details of how I dealt with both my psychological demons and the messiness of the calculation. At the end of the day, it seemed that we were paying about $15 per month more in electricity as a result of our faulty refrigerator, and with that information I was ready for the next steps.

Steps 2–4. In thinking about the future possibilities, I thought about—and projected—the purchase price of a new refrigerator (either now or when the old one died) as well as the electrical costs of each in the coming years. In terms of actual numbers, new refrigerators comparable to our current model were running about $1700 at the time. Assuming that the current one had eight more years to live and that the price of refrigerators goes up at 2–3% per year, a new one could be expected to cost about $2000 when the old one died. The Present Value of $2000 payable eight years from now is, as we know, much less. But to actually compare Present Values, we need to perform step 4 and choose a discount rate assumption (taking into account all the factors we previously talked about). As I have mentioned previously, finding your personal rate of discount (i.e., how to weigh the future vs. the present) is an important step in using Present Value. In this case, because it was only money (and not a lot of it) that would otherwise stay in my savings account (vs. being spent on something else that I valued), I only cared about how much I could earn on the money if I didn't spend it. As a result, I chose a discount rate of 5% (what you could earn on bank CDs at the time).

Step 5—do the numbers. In chapter 4, we will describe the technique for doing this calculation (this was one of those cases where an actual calculation was required), but the important part of the result was that while the value today of waiting to buy a new refrigerator after the old one died was less than the $1700 it would cost to buy a new one immediately, the Present Value of the extra electricity costs associated with waiting more than offset that difference.

For those that are interested, the following is how the actual calculation went. Using our 5% discount rate, the Present Value of buying a new refrigerator eight years from now was $1353, while the Present Value of the extra electric bills that I would have to pay if we waited until the old refrigerator died was another $1163.

Adding the two together ($1353 + $1163), we get a total Present Value cost of holding on to the old refrigerator of $2516. Given that $2516 is much greater than the $1700 a new refrigerator would cost, the conclusion was inescapable. As usual, my wife was right and we *did* need to go appliance shopping.[6]

This was a simple example (albeit one that required a little bit of arithmetic) because the alternatives were clear, the money impact was (mostly) measurable, and there was very little uncertainty about the future. Most of the situations we will discuss require less calculation, but are not quite as clear when it comes to some of the other steps in the process. Let's now look at a couple of others.

A "Once in a Lifetime" Opportunity?

If you are like me, your mailbox, telephone, and e-mail are constantly inundated with marketing offers that seem too good to be true. From offers to switch cable companies to "free" home inspections, blowout sales at your local "big box" store, and Groupon deals, it seems that we go through life spending far too much money on the things we need and if we just took the time to read and act on all these "once in a lifetime" opportunities, we could improve our financial situation considerably.

Many of us are either so suspicious or have become so numb to sales pitches that we just refuse on principle to even investigate the offers. Others respond when the offer hits a chord within them or happens to come at a time when they are looking for exactly the service that is being presented. More often than not, when we do respond, we are disappointed in the results, but there *are* exceptions, and using Present Value can help you separate the winners from the losers.

To see what I mean, consider an offer that arrived in my mailbox a while ago. It came in the form of a bright yellow flyer from a local heating and plumbing company telling me that for $89.95, a licensed expert would come to our house and clean all the heating vents/air ducts and inspect our furnace. They would come at my convenience and there would be no further obligation. Since the last time we had our vents cleaned it cost about $300, this was an offer that caught my attention. However, before I made the appointment and began to use Present Value in earnest, there was one other important factor I needed to consider.

Specifically, I needed to determine whether this was a legitimate offer and, if so, *why* was the company providing such a deep discount. This is an important question in almost any special offer that arrives unsolicited, but in this case I had not only heard of the company (they were a company we had called previously to repair our furnace), but given that the offer came during a period when the economy was in recession and contractors of all sorts were struggling to find work, it seemed very likely that this promotion was driven by the company's need to generate new business and utilize its otherwise idle employees.

So with that threshold question addressed, I started to think about the question from a Present Value perspective.

Starting with step 1, I had to decide whether or not the vents needed cleaning at all. Just because I was getting a $300 cleaning for less than a third of the normal price didn't mean I should buy the service if the vents were not dirty. So I looked back and it turned out that our air ducts had been cleaned about three years previously. A quick Internet search indicated that cleaning is recommended every four to six years, so while a cleaning might improve things, we weren't quite due. So now I knew my choice— get the vents cleaned now or wait two years to get them cleaned when they were "due."

Step 2 was also fairly straightforward. When I considered that within the next couple of years (as long as I didn't sell the house) I would need to have the vents cleaned, the future possibilities were only two—pay $90 now or pay $300 two years from now (assuming that there wouldn't be a similar deal offered at that time).

Jumping ahead to step 4, I realized that even though my personal rate of discount is high, it's not that high and so clearly getting the cleaning done now was the right move.

But you may ask, weren't there other possibilities to consider in step 2, and what about step 3? Well, in step 2 above I did consider the possibility that I wouldn't need the vents cleaned (if I didn't own the house) or that it might not cost $300 in the future, but I essentially assigned these possibilities a "zero" and that is sometimes what happens. You imagine those different possibilities but then *consciously* decide not to include them in your Present Value calculation. This is one of the reasons that using Present Value can be a lot simpler than it might appear—once you imagine the possibilities, you will find yourself eliminating some of them from consideration either because they won't affect the calculation too much (they have similar values) or they are too unlikely and therefore should be completely discounted.

The mathematically astute among you may point out that I have oversimplified things a bit in that if I were to get the vents cleaned now I would have to get them cleaned again two years sooner than otherwise (i.e., five years from now vs. seven if I stuck to the original vent cleaning schedule). While true, it turns out that that has only a minor impact on the calculation and is even less important given all the other uncertainties (e.g., I actually might sell the house in the next five to ten years) about our future vent cleaning needs.

I was now almost done, but there was another factor to consider and that was the value of my time. By having the vents cleaned, I would need to find a day I could work from home and then spend an hour or two watching and supervising the contractors as they turned the house into a chaotic noisy mess while they did their job. This was a non-trivial factor, as I value my time considerably. But even if I priced the time as worth $100 (i.e., more valuable than the $90 out-of-pocket cost), then the question still became how much more is the value of the time today ($100) than the Present Value of the time two years from now when the vents would normally be cleaned. Even at a very high discount rate (e.g., let's say we discount by one half and consider the future time worth $50 today), this factor was not enough to offset the monetary savings.

In the end, I did have the vents cleaned, but there was a final question to consider. Remember, the contractor was not making this offer just to clean vents. In fact, at $90, the company may have even been losing money on the deal. What they were really interested in was selling me more services. They were hoping (planning?) to find other problems when they saw my heating system that would allow them to obtain other more profitable business, which would offset any money they lost on the vent cleaning. Like most of us, I completely discounted this factor. First, if they did find something that truly needed doing, I would want to know (and could get a competitive bid on), and if they tried to sell me something I didn't need, I could always say no. This last point may seem too obvious to mention, but as we will see in the next example, assuming you will always act rationally can be dangerous indeed.

A Dream Vacation

My wife has always wanted to go to Hawaii. Maybe it was growing up in the Israeli desert, or maybe it was watching Hawaii Five-0 on television as a child, but whenever the idea of planning a trip comes up, websites depicting volcanoes, luaus, and lush Hawaiian landscapes will mysteriously appear in the browsing history of our computer, and whenever our future vacation destination wish lists are discussed, Hawaii floats to the top of hers.

One night we had just finished dinner and were having just such a discussion when the phone rang. We have a policy in our house of not responding to telephone marketers, but when the caller mentioned Kauai, it just seemed like too much of a coincidence, and I suffered a moment of weakness. The proposition was one that we have all heard many times before.

"Come and enjoy our beautiful resort for an incredibly low price. All we ask is that you listen to a brief 90-minute presentation about the benefits of vacationing with us more often." Sound familiar?

I had always assumed that Time Share deals were one of the worst scams out there—a bait and switch on what you get up front, a painful, inconvenient high-pressure sales pitch to endure, and since no one except a true "sucker" would actually buy the Time Share and the marketing people had to be making some money somewhere, it just couldn't be worth it. But this time I decided, perhaps as much out of curiosity as anything, to try and really understand what was going on in this business.

It turns out that the up-front bait was pretty attractive and dovetailed perfectly with our vacation goals—five nights at a one-bedroom suite at a high-end Kauai resort including lots of extras (a free car, one dinner, a bunch of continental breakfasts, as well as $200 worth of credit at various shops at the resort) all for $899. There were no restrictions on when to schedule the trip and some flexibility on when to schedule your ninety-minute "tour" of the facilities.

To take advantage of the offer, we paid our deposit ($300) and then tried to schedule our trip. Our first choice of dates was not available (according to the reservations operator we had not acted "quickly enough"), but we were able to get our second choice about nine months later—so far, so good. Even discounting heavily, the up-front deposit only added a little bit to the cost of the vacation, but things got a little more complicated when it came time to make our plane reservations (not included in the deal). Here, because we now had no flexibility in our dates (we needed to book and confirm the hotel before buying plane tickets), we ended up spending more (about $2000 vs. $1500) on getting to Hawaii than we otherwise would have.

So, let's see where we are from a Present Value perspective. The original price was $899, and the cost of the plane tickets was $2000, so to this point the cost of the vacation was a little less than $3000. Of course this was not the total cost of the vacation, as when we arrived there would be incidentals, meals, and the inevitable shopping we would do. I estimated this to be about another $2000, for a total vacation cost of about $5000. Not bad for a week in Kauai for a family of three, but now I had to determine, from a Present Value perspective, *how good* a deal it really was.

In other words, it was time to begin our five-step process. Starting with step 1, I first had to "clarify the choice." Specifically, it was important to note that had we been going to a place that we wouldn't have ordinarily gone to, this step would have been very complicated indeed as I would have had to consider the $5000 versus all the other possible vacations we could take with both their financial and non-financial aspects. But in this case, the choice simply came down to whether to go to Kauai now and listen to the Time Share pitch or should we defer our trip to Kauai to sometime in the future.

The importance of the above should not be underestimated, and it alone could have tilted the Present Value calculation against the trip. Too many times, when we look at "deals," we only compare the price/value of the product or service offered to how much that same product/service normally costs. Any deal needs to be compared to all of the alternatives, which might include either a different product/service or *not buying at all.* In our case, it was much simpler in that I knew that eventually we were going to go on a Hawaiian vacation. That I didn't know *when* that vacation would happen is important, and I did need to factor that into the calculation, but at least I didn't need to compare the price of our trip to a dozen others we might make. As noted, while we almost certainly would eventually go to Kauai, it would most likely have been a year or two later than when we went, and so after figuring out what the trip would cost in the absence of the Time Share deal, I needed to determine its Present Value and compare it to the $5000 I was about to spend. This is where step 2 began.

When I did my research on the cost of going to Kauai on our own (including the lower-priced plane tickets, but higher-priced car, hotel, etc.), it seemed that it would cost us $7000–$8000 for a comparable experience (without having to hear the sales pitch). Step 3 was—as in the prior example—very simple. Here I assumed that it was a certainty that we would be going to Kauai and proceeded on to step 4.

In step 4, I decided to use a relatively low discount rate because I was not in *that* much of a hurry to get away and as a result came up with a figure of $6500 (the value today of the $7000–$8000 I was going to pay when I eventually did go to Kauai) to compare to the $5000 that we were going to pay. Thus, it seemed that we were essentially being offered $1500 ($6500 – $5000) to spend ninety minutes of our vacation listening to a sales pitch that we had *no* obligation or reason to accept. A few months later, we boarded our plane fully satisfied and proud of being savvy consumers who were about to take advantage of a large corporation that didn't seem to be aware of the value they were "giving away." But while the decision may have seemed like a "no brainer" from a Present Value perspective, things got a bit more complicated once we arrived in Kauai.

When it came time to actually listen to what the Time Share salesmen had to say, we quickly realized that we had seriously underestimated our ability to resist or even think clearly about what we were hearing. Softened up by three days basking in the Hawaiian sun and fragrant breezes wafting through the resort, our defenses were down, and the rationale for buying a Time Share seemed downright compelling. The idea of never having to pay another hotel bill *and* being able to go almost anywhere in the world (taking advantage of the reciprocity arrangements with other Time Share owners) *and* having equity to eventually sell (maybe even at a profit) *and* all the extra *right now* benefits (another discounted vacation between now and closing, extra discounts for the remainder of our stay, etc.) was just disorienting. They told us we had come at *exactly* the right time and that, as times were tough, the manager was allowing them to offer extra special incentives if we committed right then and there. In fact this was only a *very temporary* opportunity as they were only three sales short of their quota, and there were another ten conversations going on right then, and as soon as they met their quota, the deal would revert back to the already generous (though not *quite* as generous) terms that were originally put forth.

On and on and on it went. In some ways, my belief in Present Value was working against me. The numbers just made too much sense. I forgot one of the most important principles of Present Value thinking, and that is to *take your time,* to not let your desires cloud your evaluation of the future, and to stay unattached to any particular scenario of the future. In the end, it was my wife that saved us. She is a psychologist, and when the salesmen kept refusing her request to "sleep on it" and give an answer the next day, the alarm bells went off and she dug her heels in. We were *not* going to sign anything until/unless we had a few hours to consider it.

They finally agreed to give us the rest of the afternoon and when we were by ourselves, the fever broke, and we realized that we had narrowly averted a serious fiscal mistake. All kinds of obvious flaws in the rationale became apparent. Not only was the range of alternative future vacations we might want to take far broader both in terms of location and in experience than were available through the Time Share (i.e., all the reciprocal properties were at resorts in big cities or "attractive" destinations), but the timing of these future vacations was both farther in the future and much less certain than we had been convinced of. Beyond all the non-financial drawbacks that we now saw, the fact that the commitment required tens of thousands of dollars up front meant that the Present Value of the deal was not as good as it seemed. For example, just considering the equity that we would have been obtaining, we realized that to take advantage of all these future vacations (a key selling point) would require us to wait decades before selling, and it was not at all clear whether the Time Share would be worth anything at that point. And even if it was, the Present Value of that equity cash in would be only a fraction of the price we paid.

At the end of the day, taking a step back and using Present Value to say no ultimately allowed us to get a great deal on a trip we always wanted to take and kept us from making a very costly mistake.

Before we move on to some of the more serious decisions we make in life and how Present Value can guide us to the right path, I would be remiss if I didn't mention probably the most prevalent kind of decision we face regularly, and that is whether to spend money on something we want now or to save that money for something (often far) in the future. Many of my colleagues in the actuarial and financial services industry make their living advising people on their savings and investing strategies, and in this book I have consciously avoided dealing extensively with those questions. There is no doubt that Present Value is integral to those decisions, but there are hundreds of books already written on the subject (e.g., on how to plan for retirement, get out of debt, save for the future, and get rich on real estate), and I wanted to focus on what I think is a relatively unknown aspect of these and many of the other decisions that we face.

Later on, I will talk about the one author (who happens also to be an actuary) that I would recommend reading to get better at your savings and investment strategy,[7] but for now I would just leave you with the message that Present Value thinking can be applied to any financial decision where the alternatives are clear and the consequences of choosing one path over another are measurable and, if not predictable, can be imagined— both in terms of magnitude and in timing. My intent is not to tell you whether you should take that bonus that you just got and spend it on a new car, pay down your debt, or put it all in to your company's 401(k) plan, but rather equip you with the tools to make that decision for yourself using the power of Present Value.

Chapter 3

MAKING BIG DECISIONS

Sometimes the decision is minor and the calculation is as straightforward and clear as the ones described in the last chapter, but sometimes there is a lot more at stake than just the cost of a new appliance or where to go on vacation. In many of these more important decisions, there are many more factors to consider and more uncertainty about the future, which makes the determination of what to do more interesting. It is in these complex but vital areas where the power of Present Value and its application in our day-to-day lives begins to show its true worth.

Some of the most important decisions in our lives revolve around whether to make a major purchase or financial investment and, as I said before, these clearly could benefit from a Present Value analysis. In chapter 2 I showed how basic Present Value thinking can help you navigate your day-to-day life and decide among actions whose financial consequences are straightforward to imagine. Most of the major financial commitments that we consider can be looked at in the same basic way as I looked at my refrigerator purchase and the other more investment-oriented examples described earlier. In most cases the only difference is that the dollars are bigger, so the amount of energy you put into the analysis should also be greater.

There are also some important decisions that even though they have little or nothing to do with money (medical decisions, dietary and lifestyle choices, etc.), can and should be looked at from the perspective of Present Value. We will spend all of chapter 11 and some of chapter 12 discussing decisions where money doesn't matter at all, but in this chapter I want to turn to two other types of decisions that are extremely important to both our financial and emotional well-being and that almost all of us have to face at least a few times in our lives. Those two areas are career choices and when to invest in your own education. For both of these kinds of decisions, I believe using Present Value can make a huge difference in the quality of the choices you make and hence the quality of your future life.

What follows are two examples that illustrate just how powerful Present Value can be when used appropriately and how equally confusing it can be when used in the wrong way.

Changing Jobs

The first time I changed jobs (and to a lesser degree every time I made a career move), I made my decision, in part, because I judged that the Present Value of my future earnings would be higher if I left than if I stayed where I was. I say "in part" because there were other reasons to change, as there almost always will be for all of us. I'm also not saying that no one considers the financial aspects of competing job offers. People do. In fact, sometimes it's the only thing they consider. But, even when money is the issue, most only consider the immediate financial impact of the change, or perhaps decide to leave because they have some vague sense that the new job might offer them more potential for future growth. Without being overly prescriptive, I believe almost everyone could benefit from taking a more systematic approach when considering a career move.

For me, the first time I was faced with such a choice was a little more than two years into my tenure in the insurance world. I was on a fast track. I had passed a few actuarial exams, impressed some senior actuaries, and was tagged by management as someone to "watch." In short, my prospects for future salary increases were bright. In addition, virtually all of the top positions in the Company (CFO, CIO, etc.) were held by actuaries, so there seemed to be some chance that I might rise to a very high-paid position.

Some insurance companies are run by salesmen, a few by underwriters, but most are run by actuaries.[8] Actuaries founded the industry,[9] and to this day I believe that all young actuaries interested in becoming high-level executives have a higher chance of attaining their goal at a large insurance company than in any other business. And the rewards of attaining such a level are substantial with total compensation running well into the millions of dollars. So why did I turn my back on this bright future and choose instead to join a consulting firm? Simply put, I looked at the future scenarios, considered the likelihood of each occurring, and then tried to put a Present Value on each possibility. Specifically, two years into my career I was offered a job by a major consulting firm and—while I had no doubt that I wanted to become an actuary—I had to decide what kind of actuary I wanted to be.

The choice was clear and so step 1 was not an issue, but steps 2, 3, and 4 were both critical and tricky. Starting with step 2, I tried to imagine the possible futures associated with each path. First, I looked at the actuaries within the insurance company who were about ten to fifteen years older than me, those that ended up in senior management, those relegated to technical backwaters of the company, and those that were just bouncing around from one operational job to another (noting also the number who had disappeared completely, having been let go by the company). I knew that each of those roles entailed very different streams of future income, and so the critical variable to think about was the possible paths that awaited me in the insurance world. Two things struck me as I looked at the very successful actuaries in the company. The first was that they were all very disciplined, hard-working types who had directed their efforts to getting to the top right from the beginning. This suggested that pursuing this path would entail a considerable near-term investment of time and energy on my part. The second, far more troubling thing I noticed was that for every senior level actuary, there seemed to be about three or four others who had almost the same characteristics but hadn't been tapped for senior management, suggesting that there was an unpleasant degree of randomness in determining who got the prize and who didn't. It may be—and probably was—the case that there were concrete factors (e.g., personal relationships and ability to think strategically) that drove the decision. However, since I couldn't determine the relevant characteristics (let alone whether I had any of them), I figured my best bet would be to treat these unknown factors as random and just assume that if I wanted to become CFO there was an 80% chance I wouldn't get it even if I gave it my fullest effort.

Turning to the other alternative, to leave the insurance world and become a consultant, the analysis was much easier. Almost all successful consultants followed the same track—pass your exams, pay your dues, and become a partner. The typical consultant's earnings stream was relatively steady and somewhat higher than the nonmanagement actuaries at the insurance company for a while, but then after eight to ten years, assuming that one became a partner, one's compensation jumped a bit and settled in at a very comfortable level (perhaps $200,000–$250,000 per year in 2012 dollars). The biggest variable was how quickly one could obtain partnership, but even that did not vary by much more than two or three years up or down.

In addition to the fact that consulting appealed more to me at the time and that the near-term effort required to become an insurance company CFO seemed quite a bit greater than what I would need to do to become a consulting firm partner, almost no matter what discount rate I chose in step 4, the Present Value of my compensation if I left was far greater than if I stayed for two reasons. First, after discounting the seven-figure CFO salary by the probability of attaining it, its expected value was relatively modest and second, the fact that I would have to wait so long for that payoff at the insurance company versus the potential near-term attainment of partnership at a consulting firm meant that the Present Value of this big payoff was even less.

We will talk much more about step 4 and determining a personal rate of discount in chapter 8. We have already talked about this essential idea, but just to review, let's remember that some of us would rather have $500 today than a promise of $1000 payable three years from now, while others will demand $800 for the same promise. The important thing is to be clear in your own mind as to how to equate the two for *yourself.*

Needless to say, though I have no idea if I would ever have become CFO had I stayed in the insurance world, I believe I made the right decision and have never regretted my choice. Furthermore, even in those times when I do wonder about life in the corner office, I take comfort in the fact that I made my decision in what to me was the most rational manner available given the information I had.

But can using Present Value mislead you? Absolutely, and this next story illustrates that.

Investing in Your Education

About twenty-five years ago, a friend of mine came to me with a problem that he thought called for some Present

Value analysis. It seems that his wife, Elise (a young and successful analyst for a large finance company in Los Angeles), was on the verge of deciding to quit her job and enter an MBA program 3000 miles away in Philadelphia. To him, this seemed like absolute madness. Putting aside the disruption to their lifestyle, the extreme hassle of traveling back and forth across the country (they would become a bi-coastal couple), and the delay in their plans to start a family, he believed that the decision made *no* economic sense whatsoever, that the financial benefits of getting an MBA (the main reason she was considering business school) were more than offset—at least on a Present Value basis—by all the added expenses (school tuition, maintenance of two households, foregone income and career opportunities at her current company, the possibility of not working when their future kids were small, etc.). It was this cash flow and Present Value analysis that he wanted my "expert" assistance with.

Feeling not only compassion for my friend, but convinced that his intuition was correct, I enthusiastically started in on the project. I did my due diligence, looking into the average compensation for newly minted MBAs and their potential career tracks, gave some thought to Elise's prospects and likely salary progression at her current company, identified as many of the sources of additional expense and risk factors (upside and downside) associated with each alternative that I could think of and then sat down to figure out what assumptions to use in the analysis.

I decided that to be most fair and also to address the obvious uncertainty of the outcomes, I should not use any probabilities to discount various contingencies (like Elise's chances of losing her current job or having trouble finding a new one after getting her MBA). I would instead develop several alternative scenarios and calculate the Present Value of each. For this purpose, I equated the present to the future (i.e., used a discount rate) based on the assumption that any additional money she could save now by not getting her MBA would be invested in a balanced portfolio of stocks and bonds. Specifically, I compared the Present Value of each alternative income stream (net of expenses) using this discount rate. Like a good actuary, I created a reasonably conservative best estimate, as well as a pessimistic and an optimistic scenario, each varying mostly by the future salaries she would receive under each path as well as the time it would take to reach her maximum earnings potential. Most of the expenses were pretty easily estimated, and I didn't bother to quantify the non-financial costs/benefits associated with the move, as clearly these were already a big argument against her move. Then, just to make sure I didn't miss any possibilities, I developed a best-case and worst-case scenario. I would leave it to Elise to judge for herself what the likelihood of each scenario was.

Not surprisingly, the analysis confirmed my original expectations with the Present Value of her projected net income if she stayed at her current job exceeding the Present Value of her compensation taking the MBA path by several hundred thousand dollars under all scenarios except the best case where the values of the streams were essentially the same. Not only that, but the break-even point, where her annual pay became higher as an MBA than what it would likely be if she stayed put seemed depressingly far (at least five years) in the future, and therefore if Elise used a *higher* personal rate of discount than I was assuming (as most people do), then it would be even clearer that she should stay where she was. Feeling pretty confident that she was a rational thoughtful person, I expected Elise to quickly agree that her idea of going back east was misguided and she would thank me for helping her avoid a big mistake.

Elise patiently listened to my presentation, smiling sweetly and attentively the whole time. When I was done, she thanked me and said she was impressed with all of my analysis. She asked no questions, and though I assumed I had done my job, a few months later she packed up and headed to Philadelphia to start her fall term at Wharton Business School.

It turns out that the largest economic and financial market expansion of our lifetime was just gaining momentum, and when she graduated two years later, the investment companies came begging. Soon, Elise was running a moderately sized mutual fund, and within five years of getting her degree, she was effectively managing almost a billion dollars in assets and making a multiple of my best-case scenario. Needless to say, her income was also a multiple of what I was earning as a consulting actuary. To this day, every time I see her, she reminds me of my "expert" analysis.

So what went wrong? I think part of the answer is that I didn't spend nearly enough time on step 2 of the Present Value process—imagining all of the possible futures. I was hopelessly narrow and unimaginative in my visioning and—perhaps even worse—way too attached to what I was predisposed to believe (i.e., that the future payoff couldn't possibly justify the current investment). It is very hard to envision all the possibilities and impossible to do so when one is attached to a particular scenario. Step 2 requires time, curiosity, and an unbiased attitude—and

I had none of those. I also made a basic mistake when I attempted step 4—setting a discount rate to compare the future to the present. I made the completely unwarranted judgment that Elise should use some "objective foregone investment return" as a means to produce an apples-to-apples comparison. In fact, that factor—how much to value the future versus the present—is a deeply personal matter, and no one should presume to tell someone else how to make that judgment.

Clearly for Elise, her long-term future was far more important to her than her current compensation, and hence she was, I suspect, using a much lower discount rate than I was assuming. At one point, I asked her if she used Present Value in making her actual decision and she replied, "Of course I did; I just used different assumptions." And that is the main thing I missed—that Elise simply understood the problem much better than me. She not only could see—or perhaps sense—far more of the possibilities that would be open to her with her MBA, but also knowing herself, her intentions, capabilities, and ambitions far better than me, she was much better able to judge the actual probabilities of the possible earning streams stemming from each option and, even more important, how best to judge the value *to her* of the future benefits compared to the immediate consequences of choosing one path or the other.

This is perhaps the most important message of this book. Don't let an "expert" make your decisions for you. Present Value works—but only if you take responsibility for owning the process and doing it yourself.

I have dealt with two common types of important decisions that most us will face at one time or another in our lives, but there are many others that are equally important that I haven't addressed here, and that is because most of these other decisions have a very significant *non-financial* component. In chapter 11, we will take a look at some of the most critical and ubiquitous of those decisions, but now I want to circle back and take a closer look at Present Value and the 5-step process I've outlined for how to use it.

Chapter 4

THE MECHANICS OF PRESENT VALUE— WHAT IS A DISCOUNT RATE?

Before we move on to a detailed discussion of what each of the five steps in using Present Value entails, I want to be a little bit more rigorous in describing the term "Present Value" and then go through the basics of a Present Value calculation. Critical to understanding that discussion will be the concept of a *discount rate,* so let's spend some time talking about discount rates and what Present Value really means.

Present Value Defined—Savings Bonds and What "Discount Rate" Means

The next few paragraphs have a tiny bit of math and are more quantitative than we will generally get. While Present Value math is not at all necessary to understanding the rest of the book, there is one "mathematical process" —using a discount rate—that is required before you can actually use Present Value in your life. Fortunately, however, the math required to use a discount rate is very easy and is just the reverse of a concept almost everyone is familiar with—that of compound interest and the way money accumulates into the future.

For the reader who is interested in getting a more complete understanding of the math behind Present Value, I have included a short primer in the Notes at the end of this book.[10] The derivation of the generalized Present Value formula there will give you all you ever need or want to know about how to actually calculate Present Values. However, for those of you who just want to understand how to use Present Value in your own life, the following should be plenty.

To get started, let's try and state exactly what Present Value is. As an idea, it is actually pretty straightforward. As we have said before, Present Value is the value today of something that (may) happen in the future. So for example, if I offered you the choice between $1000 today or a promise to give you $1100 a year from now, which would you choose? Well, you might say that $1000 today is not enough because if inflation is running at 2% per year you will only need $1020 a year from now to buy what you can today with $1000, suggesting that waiting for the $1100 is the right thing to do. By this reasoning the promise to pay you $1100 next year is worth about $1080 today, which is more than the $1000 I'm offering. Note also that this is almost, but not quite the same as saying that you can earn 2% on the $1000 *risk free*. We will come back to this distinction later, but for now it is important just to note that when we focus only on how the value of money changes over time, we (in this case) get a Present Value of that future promise equal to $1080 and therefore opt to defer receipt.

Now let's explore our example just a little further. What if you said to yourself that you know an investment that you're pretty sure will give you a 5% return instead of 2%? Should you then ask for $1050? ($1050 invested at a rate of 5% will yield approximately $1100 in one year.) And what about the possibility that if you choose to wait a year, I will renege on my promise, or be unable to pay you the $1100 I promised? If there is even a 10% chance that I will be unwilling or unable to pay you next year, you should take the $1000. Here we have introduced the element of *risk* into the calculation. And note it is not just the downside risk of not getting the money because I won't fulfill my promise, but also the upside risk that with the $1000 you might find an investment that will yield you more than the 2% risk-free return noted above. Now you might say that we should ignore this last factor because any riskier investment will also come with an offsetting probability of loss (e.g., if you have a "hot" business investment that will return you $1200 next year, there might be a 15% chance that you will lose the whole investment meaning your "expected" value after a year is still 85% × $1200 = $1020). It turns out, however, that most investment professionals will tell you that if you invest in riskier vehicles (like stocks) you should anticipate getting a greater return simply because you are *willing* to take on this risk. This is a deep concept and, in my view, not as obvious as the experts suggest. We will talk much more about this in chapters 6 and 7 where we will discuss how to think about the future, what *risk* really means, and how to evaluate all the possibilities.

But to complete the picture, we need to talk about one further component of Present Value. Turning again to our choice between $1000 today and $1100 a year from now, let's say you have complete confidence in me and you have no appetite for risk. Even though you know you will earn much less than 10% on the money, you *still may want to take the $1000*, and that's because you might *need* (or maybe just want) to have the money now rather than next year. This is the "liquidity premium," or "time preference" aspect of present value. This is a mysterious and in my view a fundamentally psychological factor. It is also one that is inseparable from the concept of *time* and what time means to different entities, to an individual (or different individuals), to a corporation (profitable vs. on the verge of bankruptcy), to a government, or to a foundation (or charity, university, etc.). It is the essential component of the *personal rate of discount* I referred to in the Introduction, and it is the portion of the Present Value calculation that is often the most difficult for individuals (including actuaries) to fully understand. We saw how this aspect of the calculation plays out practically in chapters 2 and 3. In chapter 8 we will see how to go about setting your own personal rate of discount.

When I've tried to explain Present Value to people, it's the term *discount rate* that most people find unnatural and confusing, and so it's worth looking at another example of Present Value that almost everyone should be familiar with to illustrate how "discounting values with a discount rate" is just the reverse of accumulating money with an interest rate. Specifically, let's consider the purchase of a US savings bond. A savings bond is a very official-looking certificate issued by the US government, which after ten years is worth exactly what it says on the front. When my son was born, he received as gifts several of these. Essentially each $100 savings bond he got was a gift whose *future value* was $100. Notice that in this case future value is determined at one specific point in the future, and there is essentially no doubt (unless the US Government goes out of business) that this bond will be worth exactly $100 at that time. In this case, determining future value was very easy. As we have already seen, there are situations where the determination of future value is not so easy because we don't know exactly *when* the payoff will occur, *what the amount* will be when it does occur, or even a combination of both. For now though let's stay with this savings bond and turn our attention to how to use a discount rate to calculate its Present Value.

Again, Present Value answers the question, "what is the value today of something that I will be getting sometime in the future?" For the savings bond, the answer is simply the price that you have to pay to get one. Interestingly, the price of a $100 savings bond changes almost daily and will vary depending on prevailing interest rates (why this is so we will talk about shortly). Today as I write these words, a $100 US savings bond costs about $80, but a few years ago you could get one for a little more than $60, and thirty years ago (when interest rates were at record highs) the price was less than $50. Is this because the price of everything seems to go up over time? Absolutely not. In fact, back in the early 1960s the price of our $100 US Savings Bond was almost the same $80 that it costs today. So what is it that causes the price today of $100 payable ten years from now to be something less than $100? What determines that difference and what causes that difference to go up and down as the environment changes? We all feel that the price today of getting $100 in the future *should* be less than $100, as getting something *now* is always better than getting it *later,* but figuring out why and how much is not something many people think about.

Again, the basic question is "how much would we agree to pay today to make sure we have $100 in ten years when the bond matures?" To answer that we first have to ask at what *rate* will the money we set aside today grow at (the concept of compound interest that we are all familiar with). That answer of course depends on what we would invest the money in. When we talk about the rate at which money could grow, we call this the *interest rate.* This is the rate we use to project the future value of the money we have on hand today. When we go back the other way and ask ourselves how much that future value is worth today, we will call this the *discount rate.* For all practical purposes these two rates are *the same thing,* just viewed from different vantage points (we will ignore for now the aforementioned "time preference" and "risk" factors in a discount rate that generally makes a discount rate somewhat higher than an interest rate). It turns out that the interest/discount rate inherent in this example is about 2.3%. The way to see this mathematically is to see that:

$$\$80 \times 1.023^{10} = \$100$$
(the future value of the bond)

(Or, if you are curious about how to solve for the rate, r, and your math is a little rusty, $\$80 \times (1 + r)^{10} = \$100$, which yields $(1 + r)^{10} = \$100/\$80 = 1.25$, and finally, $r = 1.25^{1/10} - 1 = 0.0226$, which rounds up to 2.3%.)

In the basic Present Value calculation, this equation is reversed, and instead of *multiplying* by an *interest factor of* $1 + 2.3\% = 1.023$ as we move year by year from *the present into the future*, we *divide* by a *discount factor of* 1.023 as we move year by year from *the future back to the present*, that is,

$$\$100 \times (1/1.023)^{10} = \$80$$
(the Present Value of the bond)

That is it. The above equation, and in particular the idea of a discount rate is all the math you really need to know about Present Value and all you will ever need to understand everything I have to say in the rest of this book.

And now it's time to dig a little deeper into actually using Present Value in a systematic way to make better decisions, and in particular to examine more closely each of the five steps of that process that we identified in the Introduction to this book.

Chapter 5

STEP 1—CLARIFY THE CHOICE

If you are going to use Present Value to make better decisions, the first and arguably most important step is to be clear on what your decision is. Too many times when we find ourselves in a quandary, we ask ourselves "What should I do?" and then try and formulate a plan of action. By now it should be clear that there is another more precise question that should be asked, and that is "What are the alternatives that I am trying to choose between?"

One thing I don't want to do is to characterize Present Value as a magic bullet that can solve all of your problems. There are plenty of issues and choices we face where Present Value thinking is not helpful, but in many more cases than might be apparent, Present Value thinking can provide a systematic way of approaching decisions that leads to better outcomes. Fundamentally, Present Value allows you to compare and evaluate different alternative paths that you already see. It does *not* allow you to develop *new* answers to questions that arise.

Therefore, the first step in clarifying the choice is to make sure there *is* a choice to be considered. Sometimes you will face problems where it will be necessary to come up with creative solutions from scratch, but more often than not, even if there is no perfect solution, there will be alternatives that just need to be identified and clarified.

To see this, consider my friend Mark.[11] Mark is a classical musician/composer by profession and makes his living performing, teaching, and scrambling for commissions to compose and produce new pieces. He is not a numbers guy, and the last thing he wants to do is a bunch of calculations every time he has a decision to make. But Mark is also pragmatic and a few years ago he realized that classical music, as rewarding and valuable as it is, is a highly uncertain way to make a living and would not provide the steady income he needed to support his family. He needed a way to generate a stream of money that would not take too much of his time and yet be consistent and predictable enough to rely on in those times when the economy was down and composition gigs were hard to come by.

The business/investment he found (with some Present Value thinking of his own) was residential real estate. He began to buy little houses in very depressed markets. He bought a few in Texas and a few more in Indiana. For a while things were going well; the rental income was coming in and after paying his property manager, the taxes, and his mortgages, there was still plenty left over. The only small problem was that while his tenants were reasonably responsible when it came to paying their rent on time, they were somewhat less so when the lease expired and it was time to move out. Yes, there were security deposits, but often the tenant would fail to pay the last two months' rent and leave the house in conditions that required significant clean up and/or repairs before it could be rented out again. After this had happened to him three or four times, Mark came to me and asked, "What should I do?"

I don't know much about managing real estate, but to me this seemed like a case that just screamed out for using Present Value. So the first question I asked Mark to think about was "What are your alternatives?" It turns out that there were only two realistic ones. The first alternative was to take the tenant to small claims court and the second to simply let it go and absorb the loss. Once the choice was clarified and the alternatives outlined, the determination of which path to take was quite simple. The cost of pursuing the tenant would be about $500 in hard dollar costs and at least that much (according to Mark) in time and aggravation. The potential judgment to be obtained would be at most $1500 (the limit for small claims) and the probability of both getting the judgment *and* being able to collect was less than fifty-fifty. Combine that with the fact that the $500 would have to be paid up front and the recovery from the tenant would take at least a year and probably more, and it is clear that it made no sense to pursue these ex-tenants. Present Value helped Mark to see that each time this happened, he should let go and accept the loss. In concrete terms, what this result meant is that

Mark needed to recognize that the actual return on his investment needed to be viewed as slightly lower than what he had originally anticipated.

As unpleasant as the above realization was, it was an important insight and Present Value helped him gain it. Present Value is a great way of dealing with denial and learning to be realistic. Too many times we get locked into a rigid view of what will happen in the future even *after* it turns out we were wrong. That is what happened to Mark. He had in mind a fixed idea on how his investment was working and needed Present Value to realize that his return expectations had not fully included the "friction" associated with irresponsible tenants. When we talk about steps 2 and 3 of how to use Present Value (imagining and then evaluating the future possibilities) we will talk about how important it is to stay unattached to any particular scenario. Well, the same holds true if, as was the case with Mark, your Present Value evaluation shows you that you were wrong about the future consequences of decisions *you have already made in the past.*

Sometimes, decisions are as straightforward as Mark's decision to maximize the Present Value of his time and money by choosing among two alternatives—one of which was to do nothing—but sometimes the situation is far more complicated.

Let's say you come home from work one rainy night and find that the roof is leaking badly and water is pouring down the walls of your living room. There is a message on the phone from your tenant downstairs who says that her bathroom is flooded (a problem that may be related to the rain but certainly not to the hole in your living room ceiling). Not wanting to deal immediately with the crisis, you stop to bring in the mail. Included is a bill from your son's college reminding you that this year's tuition needs to be paid. There are various payment plans that are available, but not being ready to work through any numbers, you put it aside and open the other envelopes which include two offers that alert you to the fact that interest rates are at an all time low and now is the time to refinance. Just as you are thinking about how the refinancing might help you with the tuition bill, your wife comes home and announces that she has had it with this weather and thinks that the family needs to go somewhere sunny and soon for a vacation that is long overdue. And by the way, she also wanted to remind you that with your son leaving for college in the fall and house prices on the way up, it's time to start thinking of selling the house and moving to a smaller place in the city—just like you promised.

Maybe I'm exaggerating and you've never had a day like that, but the fact is that we are constantly inundated with financial challenges (and opportunities), and much of the time the decisions that have to be made are multiple and interrelated. Now, more than ever, you need to use Present Value. But first you need to clarify the choices.

How do you do that? Well, there is no set formula, but what I do is first try to separate and sort out the key questions, making sure to organize them in terms of *when* the costs and benefits of each issue will emerge and then identify which ones can be looked at independently and which ones need to be combined because they are so interrelated. In the case above, it is tempting to say that all the decisions are related because whether it's fixing the roof, fixing the downstairs apartment, or finding a way to go on vacation while still being able to pay for college, all of those tasks require money and since we only have a limited amount, we need to consider all those decisions together. In a very general way that's true, but I still think separating out and prioritizing the questions will sometimes make the answer to other decisions obvious.

Faced with a deluge (figuratively and literally) like the one described, different people will make different issues their top priority. For me, dealing with my unhappy tenant and the water in the living room would be the first priority. First, I would want to determine what the extent of the problem was, and how much it would cost to fix. The Present Value implications of not doing so are simply too dire to ignore as the problem, and its consequences would be immediate and potentially long lasting (loss of tenant and rental income, the destructive impacts of moisture in the house, the potential for further damage during future rainstorms, etc.). The need for a vacation is also, of course, related to the weather, but the planning for—as well as the actual—vacation would need to wait until after we knew what was entailed in fixing the roof and the plumbing downstairs. The constellation of decisions around paying for college, refinancing, and/or eventual downsizing of our real estate holdings are clearly a set of related and longer-term decisions where Present Value would play a critical role, but those choices would have to wait for another (hopefully less rainy) day.

Chapter 6

STEP 2—IMAGINE THE FUTURE

For as long as I can remember, I have been fascinated by the future and after reading my first Robert Heinlein book at age eight, I became a science fiction fanatic. For the next ten years, I read almost nothing else. It was not what I would call a balanced approach to literature, but it did expose me to a wide range of theories about the nature of time and the relationship between the past, present, and future. At various times, different paradigms felt more or less "true" to me. There was Kurt Vonnegut's theory of being "unstuck in time" (or more specifically that our lives are set in stone and our consciousness just moves through them),[12] there was the idea that multiple futures exist simultaneously (e.g., Fritz Leiber's

The Big Time[13]), and of course there were dozens of books that contemplated time travel and the ability to change the future by going back and changing the past. I voraciously consumed them all and considered each theory in turn.

In that period of my life, in all the science fiction books I read, the notion that really stuck and the one that shaped my early thinking about the future more than any other was that of "psychohistory" as described by Isaac Asimov in his Foundation Trilogy.[14]

The Nature of the Future—Chaos and the Psychohistorians

Asimov's Psychohistorians were the wizards of the distant future. Mathematicians of the highest order, they were able to understand and model on a detailed level the course of human events such that they could predict the future with certainty and more importantly, make small, behind-the-scenes adjustments to the present that would steer future history in the right direction. In many ways, the idea of the psychohistorian is no different than that of those who think that through the use of Big Data and powerful computer models we can foretell the future and, if we just tweak the inputs (e.g., by passing a law or two) we can make things come out the way we want.

I now think that psychohistory and, for that matter, the benefits of computer modeling (at least when it comes to making predictions) are mostly fantasy, but forty years ago, I believed in the possibility of psychohistorians and wanted to become one when I grew up. While I eventually let go of the idea that enough information, analysis, and insight will enable us to predict and direct the future, the basic premise of psychohistory remains for me an article of faith. In particular, I believe that actions have consequences and those consequences manifest themselves directly and explicitly in the future. That there is a high degree of uncertainty about those consequences—uncertainty that is best addressed through the use of the mathematics of probability and statistics—in no way undermines the proposition that almost all of what we see happening is deterministically determined, albeit (at least in my belief system) without the guiding hand of some all-powerful being.

Lately I have come to believe that chaos theory provides the best model for how we move from the present into the future. A detailed discussion of chaos theory is beyond the scope of this book, but for our purposes here, the important aspect about chaos is that it is a process that is *deterministic but not predictable*.[15] Whether this is in any sense truly how the universe works is a philosophical proposition that one could spend years contemplating, and I am sure that there are many far smarter than me who have delved deeply into it.

Before going on, I need to say that I completely re-spect those among you who are very religious and believe that the future is determined by God alone. I would never presume to argue with such a belief, but if you are going to use Present Value, it is important that when you think about what is going to happen you suspend that belief and instead adopt an attitude of humble curiosity, noting that while calculating exact probabilities of future events will never be possible, you *can* imagine what the future might look like and you *may* be able to estimate some relative likelihoods of future events (even chaos theory allows some short-term statistical predictions). Such estimations require careful thinking and will always be approximate, but as we will see in the next chapter it is not necessary to determine exact probabilities to use Present Value effectively. We only have to get it right enough to distinguish between the alternatives we are considering.

Thinking about the Future while being in the Present

> *"The past cannot remember the past. The future can't generate the future. The cutting edge of this instant right here and now is always nothing less than the totality of everything there is."*

> Robert Pirsig from
> *Zen and the Art of Motorcycle Maintenance*[16]

Eventually, I got over my obsession with science fiction, time travel, and psychohistory and headed off to college. While there, I was, of course, exposed to a much wider array of literature and ideas about how the world works, but the book that became my "bible" and the one that has influenced my thinking more than any other in the years since was only mentioned in passing by one of my history of science professors who put forth the proposition that much of what we think we know about the world was not discovered but rather invented by the human mind and does not, in any real sense, exist until someone creates it. He illustrated the point by reading the passage from Robert Pirsig's *Zen and the Art of Motorcycle Mainten-ance*, where the author deconstructs Newton's Theory of Gravity demonstrating that it has no more external "reality" than the ghosts and spirits that many Native Americans believe in.[17] It was an insight that hit me hard, and immediately after class I went out and bought the book. I have read it more than a dozen times since, and each time, I learn something new.

The reason I am writing about it here and now, however, is because what Pirsig says about the present and the future is highly relevant to Present Value. In this step of using Present Value, it is not so much envisioning the specific details of future events that is important as the mental attitude that is necessary to adopt when contemplating what is going to happen, and here, the words of Pirsig are particularly helpful. Pirsig—like countless others—counsels us to *be* in the present moment and that as he says above, "the future can't generate the future." I would go further and say that the future can't predict or imagine the future, either. I believe that to imagine the future, you have to be firmly in the present moment. By being in the present moment, you are not attached to any *particular* future and hence are in a better position to consider *all* of the possible futures that can follow this moment. The point is that as soon as you imagine yourself in the future, you have made a choice as to which future you will be in, and even if you start to sequentially imagine yourself living through different futures, you are going to prefer one scenario over another and that will not only limit the number of alternatives you can imagine but also cause you to be less than objective when evaluating the likelihood of each. This is not to say you shouldn't think about how much *value* you place on a given set of consequences; in fact, Present Value *requires* you to do so. But that comes later.

First you must imagine the landscape, and then you can begin to explore the territory, determining the value and the likelihood of each of the possible ways the future might manifest.

Imagining ALL the Possibilities

Of course it's impossible to imagine *all* the possible ways in which the future might unfold, but to focus on just the possibilities that seem obvious or most likely can not only cause you to miss the forest for the trees, but also lead you to make serious mistakes by discounting low likelihood events that could have a huge impact on the outcome of the issue you are trying to resolve. My friend Bob Walter and I used to talk about this a lot, both in our professional lives (Bob is an attorney who is particularly good at envisioning worst-case scenarios), and in the bar after work where conversations almost inevitably gravitated towards the two games that we each pursued to a perhaps unhealthy degree—bridge (in Bob's case) and chess (my passion).

Despite not being an actuary or having formal training in probability and statistics, Bob has a superlative intuition for probability theory and the ways things might go wrong that has helped him become an expert bridge player. Bridge is a game that rewards statistical inference, close observation of behavior, envisioning all the possible (even wildly unlikely) distributions of unseen cards, and most of all, making the "the percentage play."

Bob understands and demonstrates to a degree that is unusual even among credentialed actuaries that the range of possible outcomes of any question we are looking at is generally far wider than we imagine, and that it is critical, when facing an important decision, to take the time to use your imagination and consider all the possibilities inherent in a situation, including those that might ordinarily be considered "too unlikely to matter." He illustrated this point time and again with entertaining anecdotes from the many bridge tournaments he witnessed and/or was a part of, but to show you what I mean by imagining the future, I want to go back to the many conversations we had on the question of what taking a risk really means when playing bridge versus chess, the game that I am most familiar with.

Over the years, Bob and I compared and contrasted our two avocations extensively. On its surface, chess is completely unlike bridge in a couple of key aspects. First of all, in chess one has complete information about the situation on the board. The position is there for both players to see. This is very unlike bridge, where during the bidding only 25% of the cards are known to each player, and after the bidding is complete and the "dummy" is laid down, only 50% of cards are visible. Much of the essence of the game is in deducing and/or making educated guesses as to the distribution of the unseen cards. The distribution itself is completely random, and thus on the surface there is a very high degree of luck in the game. In chess, on the other hand, there appears to be no luck whatsoever. Each player has complete control over the move they make and the manner in which the position will change as a result. But is it really so clear? Beyond that, even if there is no luck in chess, is that the same as saying that the future is really predictable?

I always used to argue that despite the complete information and theoretical presence of an objective best move in every chess position, there is so much that is unknown to chess players as they are contemplating their next move that an uncertain future is as much a fundamental feature of chess as it is of bridge. When I contemplate a move in chess, the future is largely unknown—not only can my brain not fully contain, calculate, or evaluate all the future scenarios that might emerge on the board, but I also don't know what my opponent is contemplating, how many and which of the future scenarios he or she can envision and how he or she might react to my next move. In my view, the purely deterministic nature of the game is only theoretical, and in the end there is no qualitative difference between guessing which of my bridge opponents holds a key ace and speculating on whether my chess opponent will understand the intent behind my sacrificial attack and find the defensive resources (whose existence even I may or may not be aware of) to repel it and defeat me. It seems, if anything, the future outcome is more uncertain in chess, because while in bridge I have a way of measuring the likelihood of certain card distributions and hence make the "percentage play," in chess the probability (of any particular one) of my opponent's possible responses to my move occurring is completely unknown, and therefore one needs to ultimately envision as many possibilities as one can and make decisions based on intuition rather than calculation.

But the situation is even more complicated than that because both games are (usually) played by human beings, and the plays that these human beings make (or don't make) contain information that is often highly relevant to the decision to make a risky chess move or an "against the odds" play of a bridge hand. Beyond obvious issues like the relative strength of my opponent (which could give me a sense of how he or she will play, both in the absolute and against me), there are other questions whose answers are far less objective and have equal potential impact on the decisions I make. For example, did my opponent think for an unusually long time over the last bid or choice of card to play? Why didn't my opponent take the pawn I mistakenly left unguarded two moves previously? How important is it to my opponent that he defeat my contract by one trick (vs. two or three)? What is the impact of the result of this particular deal or game on my opponent's standing in the tournament we are playing or on who he or she might meet in the next round? Are there emotional or other factors (e.g., age of my opponent) that should affect my play? Some of these questions can't be answered, some shouldn't be considered (based on ethics), and some might be downright misleading if one relied too much on their significance. However, to ignore the presence of all this additional information and to pretend that the future is predictable or "calculable" misrepresents the situation both in bridge and chess as well as in life in general. A quick story will illustrate what I mean.

As enthusiastic a student of the game and avid reader of the literature as I am, I am also very much an underachiever when it comes to my actual chess tournament results. I have beaten a couple of experts and once or twice was able to draw a master, but by and large I lose more games than I win and my rating is only class B (three steps below mastery). I have, however, played in enough tournaments to have faced a couple of grandmasters in serious games, and each time the experience was both sobering and educational. So when

David Bronstein came to town to give a simultaneous exhibition (playing thirty games at the same time against anyone willing to buy a ticket), I eagerly signed up to play.

In chess, there are masters, there are grand masters, and then there are the super grand masters—the elite players, legends of the game like Kasparov, Karpov, Fisher, Capablanca, and a few dozen others who vie every few years for the World Championship. In the '50s, '60s, and '70s, David Bronstein was very much in that category, and in 1951 came within a hair's breadth of becoming the world champion by beating Mikhail Botvinnik in an epic twenty-four-game match (the match was drawn 12–12, and Botvinnik retained his title).[18] By the time the simultaneous exhibition took place, Bronstein had largely retired from serious play but was still ranked as one of the top 200 or so players in the world, and was fully capable of producing games of surpassing beauty and depth. But he was also old, not in the best of health, and was obviously tired from touring the country and giving exhibitions in every city he visited. And so when I sat down and made my first move, I wasn't exactly optimistic, but I had some hope that I would last long enough to enjoy the experience for more than a few moves. The game began, and having chosen an unusual opening that I was very familiar with, I was able to negotiate the first ten moves or so without incident. But then, just as the opening phase of the game ended, I suddenly saw an opportunity to win a pawn with no apparent cost.

Now I was faced with a very difficult decision. World champions do not allow players like me to simply "snatch pawns." In fact, that is exactly how they dispatch weak opponents quickly. They offer a pawn (or some other piece) as bait and then punish their hapless prey with an attack that takes advantage of the vulnerability of their opponent's position that is created by the time it takes to take the "poisoned" offering. But try as I might, I couldn't see any real danger in taking the pawn. I could see some defense I would need to engage in, but no attack that I couldn't respond to. To me, it looked like a bluff. So the judgment I had to make was whether the probability that this near world champion could see something in the position that I couldn't was so much more than the chance that his move was simply the result of age, exhaustion, having twenty-nine other games to play, and/ or an underestimation of my ability (if I couldn't repel the attack I *did* see, I would lose quickly and Bronstein would have one less game to worry about) as to justify risking a quick demise by taking the pawn. The fact that my father, who was playing in the game next to me (and is only a slightly weaker player than me), had just gone down to a quick and violent defeat did not make my decision easier.

Fundamentally, it was a determination that was impossible to quantify, and so I had to use my intuition. In the end, I grabbed the pawn as much because I wanted to see what would happen as because I thought it was the percentage play. Happily, it turned out that there was no deep, hidden reason behind Bronstein's move, and I ended up with a material advantage that I jealously guarded and nursed, exchanging pieces whenever I could, until forty moves later I found myself in an endgame still ahead by a single pawn but with so few pieces left (just a couple of rooks and a few other pawns) that despite the fact that I lacked the expertise to convert my slight advantage into a win (along with the disconcerting realization that there were now only two or three other games going on leaving me with an uncomfortable amount of Bronstein's attention), it seemed that if I didn't make any mistakes I would be able to survive and end up with a draw. Such a result would, for me, be a triumph wildly beyond any expectations I had going into the game. In fact, that is what transpired, and I left the exhibition feeling elated.

My euphoria dissipated considerably when the next day, as I was going over the game with my chess teacher, we discovered that during the endgame Bronstein had made *another* mistake that I should have been able to capitalize on and win the game. It was a continuation that, though not obvious, was one fully within my ability to see, *had I been looking for it.* So excited and focused was I on gaining a draw against this famous grand master that I never, for a minute, considered the possibility that there might be an additional future possible scenario under which I might actually be able to win my game. And that really is the problem that we face most of the time—we simply get too attached to one (or maybe several) possible ways the future might unfold.

As this story shows, it is not just the catastrophes that you should take the time to imagine, but the miracles as well. The future is vast and full of both, and until we adopt a humble attitude and take the time to contemplate all that *might* occur, we will never be able to determine how likely any particular scenario is, let alone what *will* occur. One of my friends calls it the "art of not knowing." That is where the future starts—here in the present, before we know anything.

Chapter 7

STEP 3—EVALUATE THE POSSIBILITIES

The evaluation of the relative likelihood of different future scenarios is something we all do almost every day, and many of us have to do it in our jobs. However, most of the time we are not aware that we are doing it, or we do it based on our seemingly incurable hardwired tendency pointed out by many researchers (like Kahneman and Tversky) that makes us seek out patterns and see intentionality in the occurrence of events, most often on the basis of statistically insignificant or highly biased "samples" of past experience.[19] What is important about this step in the Present Value process is that you try and free yourself from that inclination and think hard about what is measurable, what is not, and what really will give you a clue as to what might happen next. To see what I mean, let's go back to my friend Bob and another favorite subject of conversation—baseball.

You see, in addition to his expertise at bridge, Bob is also a serious baseball fan. Growing up rooting for the old Brooklyn Dodgers, he learned to hate the Yankees at an early age (apparently the two go hand in hand). Being a rabid Boston Red Sox fan myself, we bonded immediately over our common hatred for the Yankees and shared many a beer commiserating with each other over the unfairness of their continued dominance of the sport. In the course of those discussions, I came to appreciate what a student of the game Bob was with his eye for the subtle nuances that abound in both strategy and play. This, combined with his encyclopedic memory and intuition for probability and statistics (as well as his Jesuit training in rhetoric), made him truly formidable in the numerous barroom debates in which he and many of his colleagues engaged. In some ways, baseball is a perfect environment to see the operation of probability and statistics in real time and to experience the perils of projection and prediction when probability theory is misapplied and those statistics are abused. From discussions of "hot streaks" and "clutch hitters"—two concepts that Bob and I were both highly skeptical of—to making predictions (and sometimes wagers) on future player or team performance, the significance of data on past performance as a predictor of future events is as relevant in baseball as in any other field where knowing the relative likelihood of future events is important. In this area (as well as many others), Bob was a master at honing in on what was relevant, measurable, and significant in ascertaining "true" ability (hitting, pitching, etc.) and likely future outcomes.

One night, for example, we were debating our choice for the greatest control pitchers of all time. We both agreed that, to have great control, a pitcher needed to demonstrate more than just an ability to avoid walks, but also to be able to throw the ball *exactly where and how he wanted it*. We each proposed our own candidate with relevant evidence. I argued that Greg Maddux was the best, based on my observation that he was able to strike out more batters with "called strike three on 0–2 counts" than anyone I'd ever seen. Unfortunately, while this might have been a relevant statistic, it wasn't one that, even today, you can find well documented. Bob, on the other hand, came up with a much more "on target" candidate statistic suggesting that Pedro Martinez was the best ever for his overwhelmingly high career *ratio* of hit batsmen to walks given up.[20] As Bob put it, when Pedro drilled you with a pitch, you knew that it wasn't "one that got away."

This interchange illustrates some important aspects about the Present Value process. First, as I have noted repeatedly in this book, two of the key steps in Present Value thinking—imagining the future and estimating the probability of future events—are used by all of us far more than we might think. When a team's owner decides to fire the team's manager because of a recent losing streak that may or may not reflect incompetence, he unwittingly is using (or misusing) Present Value, and in particular, step 3. This need to evaluate what may happen in the future permeates all of our lives and follows us even into the bar when we sit down to watch our favorite teams play. Second, we as humans are generally very bad at intuitive calculations in this regard, and we grossly overgeneralize from limited observations of phenomena that may not even be relevant. So while Greg Maddux might very well have been one of the best control pitchers ever (and therefore have a low probability of walking the next batter he faces), the fact that I'd watched him make more than a few hitters look foolish as they watched his nasty sliders clipping the outside corner of the plate is not nearly as compelling an argument for his true ability as Bob's discernment of a relevant, measurable, and statistically significant variable that bears directly on the question. Finally, beyond the importance of finding the "signal in the noise," it is important to not underestimate the effects of pure randomness on the events we see transpiring all around us.

This brings us to one of the biggest traps that you can fall into in this step of the process, and that is to try and calculate probabilities directly and to put *specific* numbers to such eventualities. In some very limited circumstances such attempts might work, but generally, it is not only more effort than its worth, but can actually lead you into making serious mistakes.

The Expanding Funnel of Doubt

> *"When a Scotsman emigrates to England the average intelligence of both countries goes up."*
>
> A saying of unknown origin often quoted by David McLeish FFA, ASA, and CEO of Godwins Inc

The roots of actuarial science trace back to the United Kingdom, and it is there that much of the profession's philosophy, values, and long-term perspective on the future and how to evaluate it comes from.[21] As a young actuarial student studying the foundations of the science that were laid by these early actuaries, I developed a somewhat romantic image of the hard headed, sober, clear eyed, sophisticated, and cultured British actuary who I imagined to be much like an intrepid ship's captain, steering his small but seaworthy craft through the uncharted and stormy seas of risk, ultimately delivering both his cargo and his passengers safely to a distant shore somewhere in the future.

In 1989 I got the opportunity to work for an actuary who came as close as any I've met to my idealized image of that nineteenth-century, steely eyed, Old World mariner. By the time I joined Godwins—a firm that no longer exists—David McLeish had been at the helm for a little over a year. Born and bred in Scotland, David had spent the early part of his forty-year career rising through the ranks of the UK actuarial establishment, a system that even as late as the 1970s would have looked familiar to the nineteenth-century founders of the great insurance companies and consulting firms that still dominated the market. But more than a ship's captain, David was a ship designer—someone who not only focused on how to build a stable and seaworthy craft, but also what sort of navigational equipment or techniques should be employed to know where one was headed and to identify and avoid any icebergs that might cross one's path.

Like the quote at the beginning of this section, many of David's views were provocative and, at first glance, counterintuitive. However, upon closer examination, his pronouncements usually turned out to be completely logical, consistent, and, if you agreed with their underlying assumptions, almost impossible to argue with. For those still struggling with his (tongue-in-cheek) statement about Scotsmen who move to England, the key is to recognize that if the Scotsman who leaves is *both* less intelligent than those that remain in Scotland *and* more intelligent than the average Englishman (certainly a possible situation, but also one that those in England might take issue with), then the statement is mathematically unassailable.

It was in my years with David that the importance of using Present Value in the *right way* was hammered home. As compelling as David's reasoning usually was, it was often disorienting for me to hear him calmly, clearly, and very patiently point out fundamental flaws in the way most people—including many actuaries—thought about the future and factored it into their Present Value calculations. Time and again, I would ask myself, if the flaw was so obvious, why hadn't anyone noticed it before? To this day, I'm still not sure why David and his views on how to think about and prepare for the future are not particularly well known within the industry.[22]

David had a quite apt metaphor for talking about the uncertainty of the future and the dangers that lie beyond our ability to foresee. He called it the "expanding funnel of doubt," highlighting the critical point that not only do we not know for certain what will happen in the near future, but as our projections go further and further out, they get *much* less reliable, often exponentially so. This view resonated deeply with my own experience that not only were our actuarial projections for the next year or two usually off by an uncomfortably large margin, but whenever we attempted to do five- or ten-year projections of the future, we were sometimes so far off as to call into question the point of doing the projection in the first place.

As hardheaded, sensible, pragmatic, and successful as David McLeish was, and as convinced as I was of David's view of both the power and the limitations of the actuarial perspective on risk and the uncertainty of the future, the rest of the world not only didn't understand or listen to his rationale, but they rejected his entire view of what was predictable and what was not.

Fortunately, during my time with David, we were able to put some of his theories to the test.

Big Data, (Overly) Complicated Models, and Being "Fooled by Randomness"

> *"We economists are good at estimating the order of magnitude of the future economic impact of events, but you actuaries seem to have an ability to know which direction things will go."*

Andrew Abel, PhD and Professor of Finance
at Wharton, in conversation with David McLeish
and the author

By the early '90s, the exponential growth of computing power and the proliferation of increasingly sophisticated investment vehicles began to give rise to a new paradigm of thinking about the future. More and more, you heard talk of "modeling" as the way to predict the future, or if not predict, to at least develop scenarios that in turn allowed for more and more definitive quantification of probabilities of outcomes and the associated risks. I admit freely that I never took the time (and still haven't) to delve into the technical aspects of any of these models, but my intuition told me that there was something hubristic and ultimately futile in taking such a precise and mechanistic approach to divining the future, and just as these issues were becoming more and more relevant to our work, I got some indirect validation of my view from an unlikely source.

Throughout this book, I speak about some of the brilliant and quirky actuaries I have been lucky enough to work closely with, but one of the most brilliant—though not at all quirky—individuals that David and I got the opportunity to collaborate with during my time at Godwins was not an actuary at all, but an economist. It was from him and through our work together that I learned a great deal about the limitations of all the complex and sophisticated analyses that purport to ascertain what might happen in the future and therefore just how (un)realistic it is for us to think we can make decisions based on an exact evaluation of future probabilities.

One day I got an urgent call from David who summoned me to his office to tell me the exciting news that we had just received an invitation to bid on a massive project to assist a consortium of telephone companies—including all of the old "Baby Bells," who were formed when the government broke up AT&T in the early '80s—with an effort to convince the FCC that a new set of accounting rules (regarding retiree medical benefits) was going to increase company costs so much that the government should allow all the local telephone companies to raise the rates that they charged AT&T to use their lines. (AT&T still controlled all the long distance calls, while the "Baby Bells" provided local service.)[23]

Obviously it is a very different world today. Not only do most of the "Baby Bells" no longer exist, and AT&T itself is just one of several cell phone carriers, but in a world with Skype, Wi-Fi connections, and multiple cable companies providing everything from streaming video to teleconferencing, the notion that there would be one national phone system managed and regulated by the government seems downright bizarre. But twenty years ago, the old order was still very much in place, and David, who had a great deal of expertise in navigating intricate regulatory schemes (the UK system of rules governing pension, insurance, and actuarial matters is a veritable puzzle palace), viewed this opportunity as truly golden. The fact that that we had no experience working with either big telephone companies or the FCC and the fact that our likely competitors for the business were all ten to twenty times as large as our firm did not deter him one little bit.

The only aspect of the bid specifications that gave him any pause whatsoever was the requirement that the winning bidder be able to demonstrate that costs associated with the new accounting rules were "exogenous" from a macroeconomic standpoint. Don't worry if you don't understand that last sentence. I still don't. I know David didn't either, but rather than give up, David simply called up our librarian and had her research exactly what was meant, in this context, by the term "exogenous." She wasn't able to get the full answer but was able to determine relatively quickly that whatever "exogenous costs" meant here, it would only be an economist (and probably a really good one) who could make the case with any credibility that our prospective client was going to suffer from them. It was also pretty clear that for our proposal to meet the bare minimum requirements to be considered, we would need to include such a professional economist on our team. This was the kind of individual that only the very largest of our competitors had on staff.

So David made a phone call to our parent company's CEO, who happened to be an alumnus (and a very generous one) of the University of Pennsylvania. He wondered if someone in the economics department of the university might be available and interested in collaborating with us on this actuarial/macroeconomic consulting project. As luck would have it, Andy Abel, a young and extraordinarily brilliant member of the department, was both available and had a particular expertise in such matters. A meeting was arranged.

Meeting a real-life, practicing economist (i.e., the kind that makes pronouncements in *The Wall Street Journal*) was absolutely fascinating to David and me, and I believe that Andy felt a similar kick, having met very few actuaries in the flesh before. We each spoke dialects of the same language and were both concerned with how the financial future might manifest itself, but it was clear that we were coming at the problem from two very different perspectives. We, as actuaries, were focused on how the cost of benefits (e.g., retiree medical benefits) would emerge over time and impact the companies that provided them. We could also tell anyone who was interested how the benefits of one company might compare to those of another company or to the average provided by all companies in a given industry. Andy, on the other hand, was focused on a much bigger picture. He sought to understand the effect that a perturbation in the whole system—in this case a change in how companies would be forced to account for their benefits—would have on the economy in general and a specific industry within that economy in particular.

As Andy explained to us, the traditional way that economists approach such issues (and in fact the way our competitors would likely do so) was to use an econometric model,[24] which essentially is a giant computer program that attempts to model the entire US economy. The model takes a vast number of inputs (e.g., number of US workers, current inflation, interest rates, corporate earnings by industry, and factory inventories), cranks through an even vaster number of calculations, and spits out what it thinks the economy will look like in future years and what *future* indices like consumer prices, industry profit margins, and so forth will be in the coming years. This seemed to David a clear case of what he called "spurious accuracy." Knowing as we did the wild uncertainties associated with trying to predict what a single company's benefit costs might be over the next few years, and how many simplifying assumptions one had to make to do so (e.g., population growth, medical inflation, and retirement ages), it seemed inconceivable that numbers produced by the econometric models that Andy was describing, with their layers and layers of assumptions that were even more speculative than ours (our assumptions were at least based on a close analysis of the past history of the company and some knowledge of its likely future course), could be relied upon as a guide to the future. As David and I began to question Andy about how this approach could possibly produce an answer that was in any way credible, we were pleased to find out that he shared our deep skepticism for the econometric approach to predicting the future.

Nassim Nicholas Taleb expressed the basic problem with these kinds of complex models quite eloquently in his book *Fooled by Randomness*.[25] The first and most important problem with the models is that all their assumptions about the interaction of various factors and what outcomes such interactions will produce are based on past history. Don't get me wrong, one can't develop any assumptions about the future at all without considering data collected on prior events, but overreliance can be extremely misleading. It's one thing to look at death certificates of millions of individuals who happened to buy life insurance and use that to estimate the average age of death of another *large group of individuals*. It's quite another to look at 1000 historical instances of a particular economic measure (e.g., inflation rate or stock prices) and draw any meaningful conclusions about the future level of those measures or even the *relationship* of one index to another. You simply don't have enough statistically significant independent samples drawn to make any valid conclusions.

This last point was hammered home to me in 1995 when I made one of the most embarrassing statements in my career. At the request of one of my clients, a colleague and I flew to Washington for a meeting with a Congressional Committee member who was considering some proposed changes in the pension funding rules that would allow companies to withdraw surplus assets from their pension plans. The committee member was concerned that if the law was passed, companies would be able to withdraw surplus that would disappear if the asset values dropped and the liabilities increased (due to falling interest rates). So he asked us about the probability of a large stock market decline *and* a significant drop in interest rates happening at the same time. Knowing this question was coming, I was armed with reams of historical data demonstrating a clear correlation between interest rates and stock market returns. I confidently— and stupidly—told him that when interest rates decline, the stock market tends to rise and that the scenario he was envisioning had never happened in the past and our models suggested that there was well under a 1% chance of it ever happening in the future. Several years later, not only did exactly this scenario occur, but models all around the country were "refined" to more "accurately" reflect the newly discovered fact that interest rates and stock returns were not so well correlated after all.

But the problems go far deeper than merely the absence of statistical significance (a set of observations can be said to be "statistically significant" when the probability that such observations could occur simply by chance is determined to be very low). Virtually all statistical conclusions based on sampling require not only a sufficient quantity and quality (i.e., a knowledge of potential correlations or other "noise"), but also require some assumed underlying probability distribution from which the data is generated. Putting aside the interesting debates that actuaries and all scientists engage in as to what is the best representation of the process under investigation (e.g., is the underlying probability distribution normal? Poisson?), all the models that I have heard of are based on the proposition that the underlying distribution *won't change over time.* Taleb has a marvelous description of this problem when he describes a hypothetical "mischievous little kid" secretly adding red balls and pulling out black balls from a bag as the befuddled economists are busily pulling one ball at a time out of the bag, trying to use the information they get with each data point to figure out what the color of the next ball is likely to be. Taleb calls this the possibility of "regime change,"[26] and to me this problem, by itself, should cast most of the econometric models out there into serious doubt.

But it gets worse. All econometric models, and much of the projections that economists (and those who would use Big Data to predict the future) make, are based on the philosophical principle of "induction," specifically that the accumulation of empirical data will allow us to form better and better theories about how the world works and that these theories can then be used to make predictions to be tested by subsequent observations. It is the basis for the scientific method that we all learned about in school and many of us use regularly in our daily lives. In no way do I want to say that the scientific method is wrong or that induction is not a powerful and useful tool, but in my view when such a tool is available we must be careful not to try to overgeneralize its applicability and use it for purposes for which it was never intended. As Taleb points out, econometrics and economic modeling in general is particularly ill suited to the use of induction.[27] Why? Simply because there will always be an infinite number of ways to model and "explain" past observations. As a result, any new observation that isn't predicted by the current model can simply be viewed as something to be incorporated by recalibrating the model. So the modeler goes back and tweaks the parameters to produce the new observation and comes back full of confidence that he has fixed the "slight" problem in his model, not appreciating the fact that the original failure to predict the observation *disproves* the model.

Taleb illustrates the above point by making the distinction between Newtonian physics, which was disproved by experiments that led to Einstein's Theory of Relativity, and the pseudoscience of Astrology where the theory can always be tweaked and expanded to explain any observed behavior or personality characteristic that doesn't appear to come directly from an individual's initial chart. I agree with Taleb that econometrics is much more like Astrology than it is like Physics.[28] But even worse, this ability to continuously "backtest" and recalibrate one's models has led vast numbers of otherwise rational people to believe that the econometric models informing *The Wall Street Journal* pronouncements by "leading economists" regarding the likely future course of the economy are more valid than the daily horoscope, which they dismiss as nonsense.

With this as backdrop, it was a tribute to Andy Abel's brilliance and intellectual honesty that he was able to see beyond the self-delusions of most of his colleagues in the field and look at our consulting project with fresh eyes.

Ultimately, Andy came up with a creative and unorthodox approach to answering the question posed by the FCC. Specifically, he developed an analysis of the problem based on a "General Equilibrium Model"[29] that was not a predictive model at all but instead compared the theoretical states of the economy with and without the change in accounting and thus provided some insights into the likely consequences of making such a change. We, of course, had no way of validating what Andy was saying, but clearly he knew his stuff and, at least in concept, the approach did not rely on making specific predictions of future events. We were pleased to charge ahead and make our proposal to the telephone companies. With David's confident, articulate, and fully credible discussion of the actuarial aspects of the problem and Andy's reputation as an economist (as well as more than a little luck) we were able to win the assignment against an array of much bigger, well-established firms competing for the business.

How the consulting project unfolded was, itself, an interesting story that taught me many lessons about regulatory complexity, the usefulness (or lack thereof) in trying to "manage" competition and mess with the free market, as well as the telecommunications industry in general, but the most interesting (and ironic) aspect of the project was its actual result. After endless meetings, thousands of man-hours, and millions of dollars, the FCC eventually decided that Andy was right, and that the Baby Bells should be allowed to recover their cost from AT&T.[30] But before the decision could be implemented, the opposition appealed. As those appeals were working their way through the courts, the Internet and other technological advances completely overturned the industry, and the entire existing telecommunication paradigm (of one long distance carrier and a dozen local telephone companies controlling all the telephone lines) became obsolete. In the end, the original question we were addressing about exogenous costs was rendered moot as the world looked completely different than what *any* model could possibly have predicted.

While many in the industry shook their heads at the colossal waste of effort, I'm sure Taleb would have viewed the appearance of this particular "Black Swan"[31] with some amusement and not have been the least bit surprised.

From Bad to Worse

As misleading and overly complex as the econometric models described above were, things could and did get a lot worse. Beginning in the eighties and accelerating through the nineties and into the new millennium, herds of math and physics PhDs began migrating from academia into the investment world. Like a species of predators crowded out by the competition in their normal hunting grounds, this breed found the new environment quite abundant with prey and with their big brains, fast computers, and sharp mathematical weapons they soon dominated the landscape. Maybe a more apt analogy would be the coming of the Europeans to America after Columbus with their gunpowder, new diseases, and attitude that through technology and "advanced knowledge" they could extend the reach of their empire.

Actuaries with their slow methodical approaches, outdated theoretical risk models, "primitive" understanding of probability and statistics, and inherent conservatism found themselves on the run—losing business to investment banks, investment consulting firms, and large mutual funds all the while having to struggle to justify both the assumptions they used and their whole approach to risk management. Before too long, actuaries' exalted status as experts in the field of risk management began to seriously erode. It didn't help that from 1982 to 2000 the US stock market enjoyed the greatest bull market in its history,[32] making actuaries' pronouncements on what future investment returns might be (a key assumption that actuaries make every time they value a pension plan) look fearful and out of touch with the modern world where sophisticated financial engineers created and ran investment funds that could generate double-digit returns while keeping the probability of losses (at least according to their models) at an acceptably low level.

What is important is that all of these models make *specific* assumptions about the probability of future events. Not only might those assumptions be completely wrong, but even if they are right some of the time (or even most of the time), it is to my mind an unwarranted and highly dangerous leap of faith to suggest that we understand the inner workings of the engine that drives the future so well as to say that that mechanism won't change over time. This is fundamentally the same problem I have with the econometric models discussed earlier (Taleb's "regime change").[33] The fact that so many of the sophisticated investment strategies that have purported to eliminate or dramatically reduce risk have time and time again blown up, creating bigger and bigger messes (most recently during the financial crisis of 2008–9) should be viewed as prima facie evidence that there is something deeply flawed in the proposition that we can truly understand the underlying nature of the randomness that governs the future.

Unfortunately, our memories are short. The fact that hedge funds based on these mathematical models crash and burn far more often than the theory that they are based on says is possible has not seemed to slow the growth of this paradigm. Each time there is a spectacular blow up (e.g., Long Term Capital Management's collapse in 1998), it is written off as a "failure to execute," an "impossible to predict event," or some technical flaw in the model, which can simply be tweaked so that it doesn't happen again.[34]

Present Value to the Rescue— What Step 3 is Really About

At this point, you may be asking yourself why I have spent so much time telling stories about the impossibility of making predictions. I admit to being sensitive on this point, maybe because I've been asked so many times "as an actuary" why I can't predict the future (like the local hedge fund manager or the economists in *The Wall Street Journal*), but I also think that it is vitally important for anyone who wants to use Present Value to do so with a healthy dose of skepticism about *predicting* the future and an equally healthy dose of enthusiasm for *imagining* the future. There is a huge difference between the two.

So, given that, how do you perform step 3 and *evaluate the possibilities*? Well, the first thing we need to do is to take a step back and review what we are really trying to accomplish with this third step. If you remember my friend Mark's quandary about whether to go after his deadbeat tenants, you will recall that his choice was to either pursue or not to pursue legal action, and therefore his decision boiled down to which alternative produced a *greater* Present Value. That's the way most Present Value decisions work—in other words, it's about figuring out which alternative is better, not about assigning an exact number to the value of a specific choice. Therefore, when you have imagined all the possibilities, it's not the exact probability of each that is important but more the *order of magnitude* of the chances that each of the possible scenarios would occur. In Mark's case, he looked at what it would cost him to go after the tenant ($500 plus time and effort) and concluded that the Present Value of the $1500 that he might recover was less than that because his chances of actually recovering the money was less than 50–50, and probably a lot less. He realized that even at 50–50, the Present Value of what he could get ($1/2 \times$ $1500 \times$ a personal discount factor) would be not much more (and probably would be less) than the value of the time he would have to invest plus the $500 he had to pay up front. If, on the other hand, he had figured that he was "almost sure" that he could recover the money, then the Present Value determination would come down to figuring out just how high his personal rate of discount was (step 4) and whether waiting the year or two for the $1500 was worth the investment.

Unfortunately, there is no "recipe" for this step, but there are traps to avoid (as discussed above) and, most importantly, ways to simplify the problem by figuring out, as Mark did, just how precise the evaluation has to be to make a difference. Once that is done, you need to look for measurable factors (like Bob's HBP/BB ratio) that will correlate with the future events you are trying to evaluate. Sometimes, it can even be useful to look at data (not necessarily Big) from the past or similar situations that might be relevant. In the end, I find that it is best to approach this step like a puzzle. Be curious, look for clues, use your imagination, be attentive for "red herrings," and have fun with it. Ultimately, you don't need to get the right answer (in fact you will never know what the "right" answer is—things will either happen or they won't); you just need to make the right decision.

Chapter 8

STEP 4—WEIGH THE NOW AND THE LATER

Throughout this book I have talked about the need to develop your own personal rate of discount and, more generally, how making good decisions requires clarity on how much weight to put on the costs and benefits that arise today versus those that are received or have to be paid in the future. Each of us is different, and each decision has its own unique cost/reward timeline, but in *every* case we need to do three things before we can assign "values" to things that may or may not happen in the future. We have already talked about one of them, that is, determining the relative likelihood of those future events. The other two are the concern of this chapter.

First, we have to figure out what our time horizon is, that is, how far into the future is it worth thinking about. There are many reasons to limit the endpoint of our consideration of future events. Sometimes, the events are far enough in the future so that by the time they happen, our original decision will be moot. For example, when I considered how many running shoes to buy, I knew that by the time I was eighty-five or ninety, I would almost certainly either not be running or no longer be alive so I didn't have to think about shoe technology beyond that point. Sometimes, the "expanding funnel of doubt" that makes up the future will be so wide and opaque that it will simply not be possible or worthwhile to imagine— let alone evaluate—the possibilities. Finally, even if it might be relevant and we theoretically could evaluate the probabilities, sometimes we simply don't *care* what happens beyond a certain point and therefore should limit the extent of our analysis.

This last point is actually part of the second task we need to engage in when we weigh the future, that of explicitly determining a personal rate of discount. Mathematically, determining the endpoint of the time-line we consider is the same as saying that beyond a certain point, our personal rate of discount is infinite and the Present Value of events that happen that far in the future is zero and therefore irrelevant to our choice. Now let's see how important and rewarding it can be to carefully consider both one's own and others' personal rates of discount.

Finding Your Personal Rate of Discount

"There are two kinds of people in the world. There are the high discounters and the low discounters. The low discounters are always going to be fine. It's the high discounters that we have to worry about."

> Dean Ippolitto, FSA — Speaking to an EBRI (Employee Benefits Research Institute) working group on what US retirement policy should be.

"The key to a happy life is to always make those decisions that maximize the present value of future pleasure."

> Arthur (Tad) Verney, FSA — to a colleague on a beautiful summer day explaining why it was vitally important to leave work early for an afternoon on the golf course.

Each person has their own *personal* rate of discount that they use to make (mostly financial) decisions. Whether or not we are aware of it, we are constantly "discounting" the future consequences of our actions. As in most psychological processes, I believe it is helpful to everyone to make those unconscious "value judgments" conscious. Not only do we gain a measure of control over the decisions we make, but by being aware of our own personal rate of discount we can gain insights into problems and can even find "win-win" solutions to problems that would never have otherwise occurred to us.

I used to believe that the fact that most people's discount rates are extremely high and that there is quite a lot of variation in these rates from individual to individual, largely reflected cognitive errors and a failure to analyze the particular problem accurately. This impression was fortified by watching countless employees of my clients opt to receive their pensions as a lump sum or choose to cash out their 401(k) balances early, paying both penalty and income taxes rather than doing the "rational" thing and allowing the money to accumulate over time, tax free. The effective discount rate implied by these decisions was often well over 10% and in every case far in excess of what any investor could reasonably expect to earn in the marketplace. I no longer believe that people are necessarily making a mistake in their determination but are in fact consciously or unconsciously applying their own value judgments to the present and the future. About twenty years ago, I actually developed a theory to explain this phenomenon and even got it published in an actuarial journal.[35] Clever as it was, it didn't make me famous mostly because it turns out that the actual psychology of time preference is much more complicated than I suggested and is a problem that, unknown to me, behavioral economists had been working on well before I considered it.[36]

So, recognizing that, as part of our natural make-up, we each have different time preferences, it turns out that there are numerous practical and empirical issues that arise when different people and different organizations utilize different discount rates to evaluate the Present Value of different future scenarios and an enormous amount of benefit that can be gained by understanding this.

Using Your Personal Rate of Discount to Create a Win-Win Scenario

The first actuary I met when I showed up for my first day of work right after college was not my boss Mordecai, but a senior actuarial student named Tad, who was assigned to show me around and give me some rudimentary instruction on some of the tasks that I would be engaged in. With his shaggy long blond hair and laid-back manner, Tad looked like the kind of guy who would be far more comfortable hanging out in a surf shop in Southern California than being dressed in an ill-fitting suit, confined to a cubicle in a large insurance company in Hartford, Connecticut. With both California and east coast roots in his family history, he was an unusual mix of naiveté and street savvy combined with an endearing curiosity about how the world worked and a powerful intuition for math and algorithmic thinking. In fact, he had originally started his career in California but then decided to come east and personally financed a trip to Connecticut to get a job at Connecticut General Life Insurance. He was quite sure he would be hired because he knew that they had openings for eleven actuarial students and he figured that even if his chances of getting any one of the jobs was only one third, the chance that he would be rejected for all eleven was vanishingly small. Fortunately, he got the job despite his basic misunderstanding of how not all probabilities are mutually independent.

But Tad was an extremely quick study who never made the same mistake twice. Soon, the quality of the suits improved, and he was able to use his good looks, quick mind, and aptitude for elegant and efficient algorithms to become both a successful actuary and a devastatingly effective pick-up artist. While I was never able to learn anything useful from him about the latter skill, he and I became close friends who shared innumerable conversations about how to apply the actuarial perspective to living a more effective (if not meaningful) life.

One subject that was a perennial favorite in our discussions was the difference in perspective between the individual and the organization. Many of these conversations surrounded the preponderance of power that the organization had and how the individual's flexibility and nimbleness could be used as a counterbalancing force. Sometimes, those discussions focused on the potential reaction of the company to a couple of their fast-track actuarial students sneaking out of the office in the middle of the afternoon for a round of golf, but more often they centered around pay negotiations and whether and when to consider other job offers. Ultimately, I decided after a couple of years to leave the insurance company and join a consulting firm, while Tad decided to build his career at Connecticut General. Even so, we stayed good friends and saw each other often.

As the years went by and our careers developed, the conversations Tad and I engaged in became more philosophical and ranged more deeply into the nature of time and money. The basic focus was still on how differently companies and individuals look at each and how "win-win" scenarios could be developed such that each was satisfied with any resulting arrangement. Specifically, we were fascinated not just by the mundane differences in how each entity viewed a specific amount of money but also by the different ways each evaluated the passage of time both in terms of time horizons and discounting future events. As developing actuaries, we were schooled by our respective employers on almost a daily basis in how financial decisions to be made by the Company should be taken and how both the long-term viability of the company's balance sheet and its future profitability would be affected by the choice at issue. Tad was much more fluent than I when it came to how organizations, particularly large insurance companies, think about time and, as a result, in 1996 Tad and another actuary, Bill Bossi, set off on their own to put these theories to the test and formed Disability Insurance Specialists Inc.[37]

Bill was the perfect partner for Tad. While Tad did the conceptual/philosophical thinking and cooked up the algorithms and business model that would lead to their success, Bill provided the motivation, the contacts, and the leadership to make it happen. In addition to being a fine "big picture" actuary, he had presence, believability, a natural inclination to delegate effectively, and the ability to identify the most important aspects of any question—a vitally important skill for both an actuary and a CEO. He gave everyone around him the sense that he had things under control, even when they weren't, and as a result he was able to sell their business plan to the senior management of several large insurance companies, an absolutely necessary first step and a challenging one given the skittish and change-resistant nature of the personalities of such executives.

The opportunity that Tad and Bill chose to pursue lay right in the heart of a line of business that almost every big life insurance company at the time engaged in, but almost all struggled with—the provision of disability benefits. Disability insurance is not only a natural adjunct to life insurance but can also be thought of as an extension of retirement benefits, medical insurance, and even workers' compensation. It is a form of insurance protection that almost everyone needs and, when not automatically provided by one's employer, many people seek it out on their own. But while the demand for disability insurance is ubiquitous and the basic expertise of providing it is clearly within a large insurance company's core competency, it turns out that historically it has not been a source of profits for many insurers. In fact, it is very hard to make money at it. There are several reasons for this—some of them technical—but much of the problem is related to human nature and the difference between the way a company and an individual look at the time, risk, and money involved in the arrangement.

The first and most obvious problem comes in the definition of what qualifies as "disability." Despite pages and pages of definitions and large bureaucracies (medical, legal, and administrative) that have arisen to determine if and when an individual becomes "disabled," the determination of such a status remains very slippery indeed.[38] The second problem is that the administration of the business (underwriting, tracking, and paying beneficiaries) is costly and can substantially eat into the profit margin of a company issuing the policy. Finally, there are the less obvious but no less serious problems related to the timing of when the payments begin, how long they last, and how much reserve the insurance company needs to set aside to provide for the benefits still to be paid.

While Tad and Bill saw opportunities in addressing the first two problems, it was their belief that they were uniquely equipped to deal with the "time horizon and discount rate arbitrage" aspects of this third problem that led them to take the plunge and start their own business.

As Tad and Bill thought about disability benefits, they realized that what is most important to someone who files a disability claim is that they get paid *fast*. For the family of the employee filing the claim, the amount of benefit, or even how long the payments lasts, is not nearly as important as the fact that the benefits start as soon as possible. This is because not only (as we have discussed before) does an individual use a high rate of discount valuing those near-term payments far more than those in the future but also because the individual is not thinking about the "time horizon." Instead, individuals are most focused on the fact that they will be paid for as long as they are disabled and don't think too much about when the payments might end, either through death or recovery.

On the other hand, from the perspective of the company making those payments, the date the benefits begin is not nearly as important as the date they end. Insurance companies need to recognize as an expense (and hold as a reserve) the *total Present Value* of the claims that are expected to be paid, and that Present Value determination is based—by law—on a discount rate much lower than any rate that an individual would use. Thus, not only is the existence of those future payments vitally important to the company, but the *value* that the company places on them is much higher than that assigned by the individual. It was this difference between how individuals and their organizations valued that future stream of payments that Disability Insurance

Specialists took advantage of. Tad and Bill set up a claims administration operation that was focused on the one hand on processing incoming claims as fast as possible and on the other hand included an extraordinary vigilance in monitoring very closely the health status of the individuals who were getting paid so that those who recovered or died would be identified immediately, and their claim payments would stop as soon as possible. With these as their highest priorities, Disability Insurance Specialists was able to provide service that led to both more satisfied customers and higher profits for the insurance companies who decided in greater and greater numbers to outsource their claims administration to Tad and Bill.

In addition to other more mundane factors that led to the company's success (among other things, Tad and Bill were both great people managers who knew how to provide their employees with the right mix of present and future compensation, financial and otherwise, to keep their workforce stable and highly productive), there is one other reason why Bill and Tad are now playing a lot of golf. Specifically, in developing their business strategy, they were aware of and relied heavily on the fact that their *own* personal discount rates and time horizons differed substantially from that of the companies whose claims administration function they took over.

In particular, Bill and Tad knew what their time horizon was and had thought clearly as to what the value (to them) of profits and losses would be in all of the future years between the beginning and the end of their venture. Thus, with their flexible and nimble staffing model and no need to explain things to outside shareholders, they were able to accommodate the ups and downs of disability claim volumes that followed the economic cycle better than an insurance company for whom the time lag associated with hiring and "de-hiring" large numbers of people was very expensive. Even more importantly, by being aware of their timeline from the outset, Tad and Bill were able to design their business model around a time horizon that worked for their personal financial objectives. They did not ignore the endpoint of their business or, as most insurance companies do, consider themselves as "immortal."

As a result of all of the factors above, Bill and Tad have been able to cash in by transferring profits and equity back to some of the insurance companies that helped put them in business to begin with and by doing so have converted their success into a stream of steady and certain income that will last them the rest of their lives. Even this last deal took advantage of the difference between the discount rate used by the insurance companies to value future costs and that used by Tad and Bill to value the income they received. In short, they used a deeper and broader understanding of Present Value to create a "win-win" situation and assure their own financial security.

Tad and Bill have been attentive to their own personal rates of discount for over thirty years, and it has served them well. But you don't have to be an actuary to determine your own discount rate. Everyone has the capability to do it, and it's not that hard. All you have to do is let go of the notion that there is a "right" answer. Not only can your discount rate differ from your neighbor's, but it might also differ depending on the question, and it will almost certainly differ when you consider different time periods in the future. If the question is about receiving/paying money now versus some point in the future, it *might* be driven by how much interest you can earn on the money between now and that point in the future, but it will likely include many other factors as well.

So how do you begin? Well, after you have gone through steps 1–3 and you have some future scenarios that have values (monetary or not) payable at various points in the future, just start asking yourself questions about those "payment points." If, for example, you are thirty-five years old and trying to decide between leasing a new car for $400 per month and increasing your 401(k) contributions by the same amount, you should ask yourself how much more important is that $400 of "new car value" compared to the income that the $400 will provide from your 401(k) plan thirty years from now. You don't need to know how much income you will be getting—you just need to have a sense of the trade-offs. Would $1000 of income thirty years from now be worth giving up the $400 for? How about $2000? What about compared to the $400 lease payment you will be making two years from now? The specific answers you get are not nearly as important as becoming conscious of how you personally weigh value that you get now versus value that you get later. Don't worry if you get lots of different values depending on the choices and the points in the future that emerge.

Just like with step 3, the specific values you get from answering the above questions are not nearly important as the *relative* weights you are putting on the "now," the "later," and the "much later." As we will see in the next chapter where we address the final step of Present Value thinking, "doing the numbers" is a lot less complicated than it might seem.

Chapter 9

STEP 5—"DO THE NUMBERS"

If you have done a good job on steps 1–4, the final step in determining Present Value will usually be surprisingly easy.

Most of us are familiar with the old joke about the two guys out camping who see a hungry bear heading for their campsite. As one guy begins to put on his running shoes the other one asks him why he is bothering to do so. After all there is no way he is going to outrun the bear, even wearing running shoes. The second guy replies, "I don't have to outrun the bear, I just have to outrun you." Well, using Present Value is a lot like running from the bear. Most of the time we are not trying to determine what the exact Present Value of a particular future path is but rather whether the Present Value of one path is greater or lesser than that of another.

In chapter 4, the fundamental math of Present Value was described and, yes, in some cases it makes sense to estimate actual probabilities, determine an explicit discount rate, and plug everything into the simple formula at the end of the chapter or the more complete one in the appendix. But in most situations, all it takes is going through the *process* of steps 1–4, and the answer to step 5 will be obvious, or at least you will be able to get a "sense" of the answer, and you can make your choice with some confidence that you are following the right path.

I have tried to illustrate how exact calculations are not necessary a few times throughout this book, most notably in the Introduction when, even with no bears in sight, I had to decide how many pairs of—soon to be discontinued—running shoes to buy. In that example, after I had completed steps 1–4 of the process I *felt* (vs. calculated) that by buying all the pairs in stock at one store (i.e., four pairs) the "Present Value of my future running experience" minus the price I paid in dollars (about $200) would be both higher than zero (the Present Value of buying nothing) and higher than the Present Value of buying more than four after factoring in the cost of those extra shoes, the fact that the use of those extra shoes would be farther in the future (and hence less valuable), and the additional time and energy it would take to go to other stores to get them. I certainly could have bought a single pair (or two or three), but with the expectation of using all four pairs within the next few years and the fact that there was no extra time involved in buying the extra pairs, the decision seemed relatively clear.

You could say that in this case, I "went with my gut," and while that is true, having gone through the thinking process involved in steps 1–4, it was a much smarter "gut" than it would have been without Present Value thinking. As I hope the following story shows, it's developing that "smarter gut" that is the true goal of Present Value thinking and not learning how to do detailed calculations every time you have a decision to make. When it comes to Present Value, it turns out that once we are familiar with all the relevant factors, we are often much smarter than we think we are.

Learning to Outrun the Bear

> *"All you need is to keep an RPA (i.e., Relaxed Playful Attitude)."*
>
> Charlie DeWeese, FSA, explaining to the author how it is possible to complete a 100-mile road race (and anything else that seems impossibly hard)

My first boss, Mordecai, taught me what Present Value *is* and how it can be found almost everywhere, but it was from my second boss, Charlie, that I learned *how* to calculate it, or more specifically, *when* you need your calculator and when and how to use other means to get to the answer.

When I started working for him, Charlie was not yet forty and still over a decade away from running his first ultra-marathon. Yet, even then he was already a legend within our company and on his way to becoming one within the profession. Without a doubt, he was the smartest guy I ever worked for, and unlike me, he *did* pass all ten of his exams on the first try, even doubling up (taking two of the three-to-six-hour exams in the same exam session) two or three times throughout the process.

Even more impressive than his exam record was the fact that he was the only person I know who solved Rubik's Cube from scratch—with no advice, no math, and not even a pencil and paper to assist. All he used were his hands, his eyes, and his brains. The first time he solved it, it took him a week of twelve-hour days. The next time it was three days, then one day, and then pretty soon he was able to put the cube back together within a matter of minutes. But, like everything else about Charlie, his method was just a bit unorthodox. He claimed that as complete and effective as his algorithm was, it contained three "secret moves." These were moves that his hands knew, but not his brain. So his approach was to manipulate the cube until it reached a state where it was ready for "secret move number 1," at which point he would turn the cube over to his quick-moving hands only taking back control when the hands were done with their business. Then he would begin working toward the position that called for "secret move number 2," and then on to "secret move number 3," after which he and his conscious brain could finish up the puzzle.

Needless to say, Charlie marched to very different internal music than the rest of us. How different, particularly when it came to evaluating risk, was apparent from the very first day we met. It was a hot humid late summer's day, thunderstorm season in Hartford, and as we sat in Charlie's office discussing my new role on his team, we could see the sky beginning to darken ominously. While I gazed out the window with only moderate interest,

Charlie began to get excited. As it became clear that this was going to be an intense storm, Charlie began packing his stuff and told me we would have to cut short our discussion, as he had to go. Thinking that he simply had to run out because he'd left the windows on his car open, I offered to stay put until he returned. He looked at me with a mischievous smile and said "Don't you understand, this is the *best* possible weather for wind surfing—I've got to get my board and get to the lake before this front passes through!" And so one of my very first images of Charlie was that of an outwardly normal businessman racing out and disappearing across the company parking lot at two in the afternoon with the wind howling and lightning flashing to go test his skill and the fates in a manner that seemed absolutely incomprehensible.

Now, the specific unit I was assigned to was a small special secret team that Charlie had been asked by the CFO (Bill Taylor) to form to analyze potential acquisition targets that the company wanted to consider. Bill had known Charlie since they were actuarial students together, and while Charlie spent his actuarial youth solving mathematical puzzles and learning to dodge lightning bolts, Bill was the consummate focused, ambitious, old-school actuary who quickly rose through the ranks and within a few years became one of the youngest CFOs in the industry. Bill's genius was to surround himself with the smartest people he could find and tap into their skills and intelligence to achieve objectives that would be unattainable on his own. And Charlie was someone whom he kept particularly close. Personally, I found Bill scary, not unlike a small grizzly bear that you wanted to keep well fed. He didn't say much, but his questions were always unexpected and piercing, and he had intense otherworldly blue eyes that, when turned your way, felt like they could see right through you. Charlie, on the other hand, knew just how to handle him and was able to essentially spend his days pursuing whatever interest caught his fancy as long as he was available and present when Bill needed him.

The work itself was fascinating and unlike anything I'd ever expected to get involved in when I signed up for my first actuarial exam. While Charlie and the other two members of the team scoured the landscape for large insurance companies that might be a good strategic fit with ours, I was set the task of finding a shell life insurance company with a particular tax status (Phase II negative if I recall), that the company could pick up for cheap and use to manage its corporate tax liability. I was given a big thick book with the legal and financial profiles of all the insurance companies in America and told to go find one that fit our needs. It was like a combination treasure hunt/detective mystery; maybe a little like the current search for an earth-like planet revolving around a distant sun with just the right physical and atmospheric characteristics to be a candidate for colonization. Charlie provided the ultimate in hands-off management but was generally very interested in what I found and was always willing to answer questions, as long as they were intelligent, interesting, and ones whose answers could lead to more interesting discoveries. That sense of not knowing exactly what to look for but striving to maintain that "relaxed playful attitude" of curiosity and interest in what was out there was a lesson I learned well and forms the basis of much of what I believe it takes to use Present Value effectively.

But perhaps the most important aspect of Present Value that I learned from Charlie came one day when he came back from a meeting with Bill about some big property and casualty company he was proposing we look at (our company specialized in life insurance). Bill had given him a question about some present values that were buried in the target's financial statements and Charlie was struggling with how to answer it. Typical of Charlie, he was able to transform the question into an elegant and compact mathematical equation that he then gave me to solve. Unfortunately, it was a fiendishly difficult equation that did not seem to lend itself to any of the normal actuarial techniques I'd learned. Assuming that Charlie was anxious for the answer, and not having any better approach, I started expanding the equation, manipulating terms, and transforming it in any way I could. Eventually I was left with a horrible mess, but at least it was a mess that I had some access to. I was able, laboriously and tediously, to get a numerical answer for one piece, a pretty good estimate for another, and an argument that seemed to suggest that the residual unsolved portion was relatively insignificant compared to the answer as a whole. With some trepidation, I brought my now several pages of work to Charlie.

I could see from the moment I began to go through my work that I was in trouble. Charlie's first reaction was one of dismay and discomfort, much like one would react to being served a plate of rancid meat. But, even worse, the longer I went on, the less interested and apparently more bored did Charlie get. He asked me, "Are you sure there is no easier way to solve it?" and when I said "No," he said, "Well let's forget it then." He didn't even want to see my final result, and to this day I don't know what he said to Bill.

From then on, it was obvious to me what I needed to do to make Charlie happy. Whatever the problem was, my job was to clarify and make things simple, not to make them more complicated. Beyond that, I learned that if you get bored with the answer, then your audience will as well, and the answer itself becomes useless. The application to actuarial problems in general and Present Value in particular was clear. You should strive for elegance, always keep an "RPA," and use everything in your power to get the right answer, whether it be your knowledge, your memory, your imagination, or even the secret moves that only your hands know how to make.

Chapter 10

PRESENT VALUE FOR ORGANIZATIONS AND COMMUNITIES

In chapter 8, we touched on not just how individuals use Present Value but also how organizations do so. In fact, managers at many companies—particularly if they have an MBA—would say that almost all important decisions a company makes utilize Present Value, only they call it the "discounted cash flow method."[39] It's true that, superficially, the mechanics of the discounted cash flow method and Present Value thinking are quite similar, but in fact there are some subtle—but very important— differences. For one thing, the discounted cash flow method generally focuses on just the "high likelihood" scenarios, while in Present Value thinking we try to imagine *all* the possibilities, recognizing that low likelihood/high impact possibilities can be *very* important. Nassim Taleb calls these possibilities "Black Swan" events and suggests that such "impossible to predict" scenarios are the ones that ultimately change our lives in the most important ways.[40] While I agree with Taleb that these scenarios are impossible to predict, I don't think they are impossible to imagine. That is why step 2 is so critical to Present Value thinking, a step that is usually given little attention in discounted cash flow analysis.

In addition to the above, discounted cash flow models typically only consider financial/measurable factors, while Present Value takes into account non-financial items. Furthermore, discounted cash flow models take a pure "foregone investment" or "cost of capital" approach to setting a discount rate. We have seen before that for individuals, non-financial factors can be extremely important, and setting a discount rate only based on "foregone investments" ignores the way we as individuals inherently value things today versus the value we place on future consequences. I would argue that both of these factors are relevant for organizations as well, and as a result here, too, Present Value should be used to make important decisions.

Many would say that an organization (company, government, community, etc.) chooses its discount rate on a more "rational" and less psychological basis, but is it really true that organizations themselves utilize a more "rational" model for determining time preference? After all, organizations are made up of human beings, each of whom, as we've seen above, does not utilize a consistent or even determinable (as yet) model for how time passes or how important the present is relative to the future.[41] In chapter 8 we discussed how "time horizon" effects might affect the decisions that organizations make regarding present and future events and the implied discount rates in the present values they come up with, but I wonder if there is more to it than that. Perhaps every organization has its own "personal rate of discount."

Even though their finance departments may pride themselves on incorporating cost of capital and foregone investment rates into their decisions, in practice it may be that organizations make decisions based on the aggregate discount rates of their human participants (or at least its senior managers). How many young high tech companies (run by extremely young CEOs) have we seen making decisions (from what products to develop, to how to compensate their employees, etc.) that imply an extraordinarily high rate of discount? How many public companies do we see focusing solely on near-term financial results at the expense of long-term stability, and how many governments do we see these days taking steps on issues ranging from the environment to retirement policy that imply a disproportionate emphasis on the here and now versus the long-term future? It cannot be that those organizations and their leaders don't anticipate being around for the long term. Clearly they do—or at least say they do.

I believe that organizations can make better decisions not only by being more thoughtful about the discount rate they use (step 4) but also by being more systematic and adhering more closely to the principles of Present Value, laid out in steps 2 and 3. Organizations need to do a better job imagining the future, then evaluate the relative likelihood of possible scenarios, *and* utilize a discount rate that reflects the appropriate time horizon and time preferences of their particular entity.

The failure to imagine all the possible futures (step 2) was illustrated by the story of the FCC and the telephone companies I related in chapter 7. Many organizations also go astray in step 3 by trying to explicitly predict the future and determine the exact probabilities of what is going to happen, and almost all of them do not think clearly enough about their time horizon and discount rate.

But there is another challenge an organization faces in making a Present Value decision. Almost by necessity, the factors involved are more complex than a decision taken by an individual. The shape of possible future scenarios stemming from the choice that an organization makes may be similar to that facing an individual, but since the effects are felt by more people to varying degrees, determining the "value" of each of those scenarios is more complex, and that value will vary considerably by virtue of the various stakeholders in the decision.

To illustrate that complexity and the distinction between Present Value and "discounted cash flow" analysis for an organization, I want to look at a set of decisions that are being made across the country right now around an issue that is both vitally important to many people's future and one that I believe is a textbook example of how the failure to utilize Present Value in the right way can lead to disaster.

Specifically, let's turn our attention to the state of our public employees' retirement programs, a subject that is very much in the news these days. Much has been written about the plight of retirees in the wake of Detroit's bankruptcy[42] and the desperately underfunded condition of the Illinois State Pension Plan,[43] but well before those plans got into trouble, there was a state where (in my view) almost all of the principles of good Present Value thinking were violated, creating a financial crisis that almost sank their retirement system and problems that are still having to be dealt with today, twenty years after they emerged.

Promises, Promises, Promises

I was first introduced to the world of public pension plans in the mid-nineties when one of the employers who participated in the Oregon Public Employees Retirement System (OPERS) asked me to take a look at the bill that they had just received for the year's pension contribution. This was at a time when the stock market was booming and the investment returns that large pension funds were able to obtain were running at 15%–20% per year. OPERS was no exception,[44] and so my client was puzzled (and not a little dismayed) to find that even with these robust returns, the amount she was being asked to contribute to OPERS each year kept increasing. Theoretically, the benefits of these investment gains should have reduced the plan's "unfunded liability" and with it, my client's costs.

It didn't seem reasonable to me either, but when I looked more closely at the actuarial report and the provisions of Oregon's Plan, the answer was obvious.

There are two kinds of retirement plans that are typically provided by states, cities, counties, and other governmental entities to their employees. The first is a "defined benefit" plan under which a fixed pension benefit (that might be a function of an employee's years of service and salary) is provided by the plan and guaranteed for life. One key aspect of these plans is that because the benefit is fixed and guaranteed, the cost of these plans is variable and depending on investment returns (and other demographic variables), the amount an employer has to contribute every year to pay for the plan goes up and down. Historically, this "pension promise" was the predominant type of plan provided not only by public employers but in the private sector as well.

Beginning in the early 1980s, more and more employers began implementing "defined contribution" plans. Unlike defined benefit plans, a defined contribution plan specifies the amount the employer will contribute to a retirement account on behalf of each employee every year, and how much an employee receives in retirement will depend on the investment returns that account enjoys. So, while a defined benefit plan provides guaranteed benefits for the employee and variable costs for the employer, a defined contribution plan provides variable benefits for the employee but guaranteed cost for the employer. Thus, when an organization decides what kind of retirement plan to provide, they have to make a decision as to how much risk (upside and downside) they want to take on and how much they want to pass on to their employees.

Even though my client thought that OPERS was a traditional defined-benefit plan, in fact it was *not*. In truth, it wasn't a defined-contribution plan either. It was *both*. The way OPERS worked was as follows.[45] The basic benefit was determined under a defined benefit formula (e.g., someone who worked for the state for thirty years and retired at age fifty-eight would receive a lifetime benefit of 50% of their final, average salary, payable until they died). However, operating in tandem with this formula was another defined-contribution arrangement (the "Money Match") under which an account was set up (though in this case not actually funded) and 12% of pay was allocated to it each year (6% contributed by the employee and another 6% "Money Match" allocation by the employer). That account would then be credited with interest each year based on the investment returns actually experienced by total plan assets (not just amounts that were actually in the account). When the employee chose to retire, the account would be converted into a lifetime annuity. The employee would then get *whichever of the two benefits was bigger.* Thus employees would get the best of both worlds. If investment returns were poor, they would receive the basic defined-benefit formula benefit, and if investment returns were good, they would receive the "Money Match." Needless to say, if the employee got the best of both worlds, the employer got the worst of both worlds.

But it was worse than that. The state provided for a minimum *guaranteed return* on money-match accounts of 8% per year. So in good years, money-match accounts would be credited with the actual return on assets,[46] but in bad years the accounts would still be credited with 8% interest. Not only was there no risk to the employee on the defined-benefit piece, there was no risk on the defined-contribution piece as well!

In retrospect, the consequences of operating a plan like this were inevitable. The plan was extremely popular with employees and as the stock market boomed throughout the '80s and early '90s, benefits soared. Even when the market paused or pulled back, the effect of the 8% guarantee kept benefits on a steady upward trajectory. Eventually, OPERS participants began retiring with guaranteed pension incomes of well over 100% of their earnings while employed.[47] But, of course, there was a price. Costs for all the employers in the state (including cities, counties, and police and fire districts, as well as municipal utilities like my client) began to increase dramatically and by the time I was called in, the annual cost of some employers' annual OPERS contribution was exceeding 20% of payroll.[48] By contrast, the employer cost for a typical retirement plan in the private sector (regardless of whether it is defined benefit or defined contribution) is generally around 5%–10% of pay.[49]

So what went wrong? How did the state get into this mess, and what would it take to get it out?

Believe me, when a multibillion-dollar mishap like this occurs, there is no shortage of "blame analysis" (not to mention litigation) that ensues, and my purpose is not to recount the details of those debates. I spent hundreds of hours helping to untangle the mess and learned a tremendous amount about both the political process and the mechanics about how public employer retirement plans operate. As fascinating as it was, it is not the subject of this book. What I want to do instead is to take a step back and talk about how a clearer understanding and adherence to the principles of Present Value thinking could have avoided much of the disruption and broken promises that ultimately occurred.

One might say that step 1 of the process was not performed well because when the Oregon Legislature implemented the plan's formula (including the money match), they did so without fully understanding the nature of the choice it faced. Instead of deciding whether to adopt a defined-benefit or a defined-contribution structure, they chose to adopt *both* types of plans. As flawed as that first step may have been, I think the problem was less with clarifying their choice and more with the Legislature not being clear on the present-value implications of the decision they faced and in particular the way steps 2 and 4 were (not) performed.

I wasn't present at the time, but I can well believe that a comprehensive discounted cash flow analysis was performed before the decision was made. Furthermore, in doing that analysis, let's say that the Legislature did enumerate the three options they might have considered: a defined-benefit plan, a defined-contribution plan, or the "combo" plan they ultimately chose. How should they have approached it? Well, as we know, in using Present Value, step 2 is critical, and to my mind, this was the root cause of the problem. In particular, I believe there was a failure of imagination. When the money match was implemented in the mid-seventies, projections of benefits were undoubtedly done (with the cash flow duly discounted), but clearly those projections did not extend *far enough into the future*, nor did they consider *a wide enough range of possibilities.*

In 1978, I can well imagine that it must have seemed absurd that interest rates would fall to the low single digits and that that, combined with stock market volatility, would cause money match benefits (and costs) to skyrocket, but using Present Value thinking, the decision makers might have been able to foresee that as a *possibility*. Furthermore, even if they considered what actually occurred as being "highly unlikely," it seems that the potential consequences of such a scenario were never fully investigated. Had such an analysis taken place, the money match would likely not have been implemented in the way it was, and the crisis that ultimately ensued could have been avoided.

Given that the promises that OPERS made (and the Oregon Supreme Court has ruled several times on just how ironclad those promises were) extended decades into the future, it was, in my view, essential to consider the impact on employees and the financial health of all the cities, counties, and so forth of what it would take to fulfill those promises in all circumstances. In this case, the results of the failure to execute step 2 were wrenching. When the full extent of the problem became apparent, all the public employers that participated in OPERS were faced with a series of very difficult choices. First they had to "stop the bleeding" and make sure the problem didn't get worse. This was harder than it might seem since participants understandably felt that they had a contractual right to all the benefits that were part of the plan when they were hired.

But fixing the problem for the future was only half the battle. By the mid-nineties, the outlook for Oregon and its local governments was so grim that if *current* benefits were not reduced for employees and maybe even retirees, basic services (e.g., fire, police, and schools) of cities, counties, and other public entities might have to be cut back to forestall bankruptcy, and everyone saw the present-value implications of *that* scenario. It was a classic case of "pay me now or pay me later," and regardless of the discount rate used, there was no option for deferring payment any longer.

Beyond the obvious importance of being more attentive to low likelihood/high impact events in step 2, there was one other aspect of Present Value that is central to the story of OPERS. I mentioned it at the very beginning of this chapter. Specifically, it is step 4. While I am sure that OPERS and their actuaries did a great deal of thinking about the discount rate to be used to determine the Present Value of benefits that were published in its report each year, I am not as sure that they thought enough about the discount rate and *time horizon* to use when considering the design decisions that led to the 8% guarantee on money-match accounts. This decision was made by individuals whose time horizon might or might not have extended beyond the next election or the next collective bargaining contract.

In fact, I would state this principle more strongly. As a general rule: *Decisions about long-term promises, like pension benefits (as well as many others affecting large groups of people), require a time horizon and a discount rate that reflects the interests of the organization or the community itself and not just the aggregation of the personal rates of discounts of all the parties involved in making the decision.*

In the end, all the parties were able to put aside their agendas—and there were many—and craft a solution that spread the financial pain and broken promises as equitably as possible. In developing that solution, the five steps of using Present Value effectively were followed much more faithfully with both the financial and non-financial consequences of system changes considered. Steps 2 and 3 in particular were better addressed with more possibilities and their relative likelihoods analyzed. Finally, unlike in the past, a much longer time horizon and different stakeholders' discount rates were taken into account.

No one was happy with the final result, but no city or county went broke, and the system survived. Today, except for limited "grandfathering" of longtime employees and retirees, the "new" OPERS is basically a defined-contribution plan,[50] and Oregon is no longer in the news as one of those states where pensions are at risk.

In my opinion, traditional discounted cash flow analysis is inadequate for use by organizations that are contemplating making a very long-term commitment like a pension plan. For this, the tool of Present Value is essential, but even here that tool needs to be utilized with skill, finesse, and most importantly, a recognition that an organization is *more* than just the collection of the individuals who make it up.

Chapter 11

WHEN MONEY DOESN'T MATTER

One of the challenges that I got from friends and colleagues as I was starting to write this book was that, to many, Present Value seemed like a very limited concept that can only be utilized when the decision being faced is a financial one. The question they posed was, if you can't translate the value of the thing you are considering to a dollar amount, how will you ever be able to use Present Value mathematics to conclude anything useful? I believe that many of the examples that I've discussed in the last few chapters show that nonmonetary values *can* be looked at through the lens of Present Value, but in most of those examples money was still the most important component of the choice. But what if money is not the main consideration? In fact, what about situations where money doesn't matter at all? In this chapter we will look at a few of those cases.

A Matter of Life and Death

"I'd rather be eaten by the Bear than hide in my cave waiting to starve."

Rob Frohlich – on whether to undergo a
dangerous experimental cancer surgery

When my childhood friend Rob and I were about five years old, my father took us to a local farmers' market. We filled the car with a cornucopia of fruit, and sitting between us in the back seat was a basket full of ripe Fuji apples. Both of us were hungry, and both of us looked longingly at those apples. It never occurred to me to do anything other than wait, but Rob reached over and began tasting the fruit. Not satisfied with tasting just one, he systematically took a bite out of each and every apple in the basket. He wanted to know what *all* of them were like. Needless to say, there was hell to pay when we got home, but almost right up until the day he died, fifty years later, Rob lived his life just like that, voraciously sampling all that life has to offer with not a single thought to the future consequences of his actions.

Even though he moved to Canada when he was in his early teens, Rob and I stayed close through high school but then lost touch for almost fifteen years. I had no idea where he was and had pretty much given up ever reconnecting until I heard a rumor that he was tending bar in a little town called Truckee, somewhere in California. Soon after that, my wife and I were in Lake Tahoe on vacation, and I realized that Truckee was just on the other side of the Lake. I convinced my wife to help me look for him, and so we headed down the town's main street intending to stop at each bar and restaurant until we found him. At the first place we visited there was no Rob, but I was quickly directed to another watering hole not too far down the road. We walked in, and there he was. He looked up and with only a second's pause said, "Hey Pete," clearly happy to see me, but not the least bit taken aback or shocked at my unexpected appearance—just simply open and interested in whatever adventure happened to be coming next. We spent the next three hours catching up on our lives.

Being an actuary does not generally lead to many adventures or exciting stories, so I spent at least two and a half of those hours listening to his. It turns out that Rob had packed a lifetime of excitement, danger, and drama into those fifteen years. From run-ins with real pirates in the Canary Islands, to sailing across the Atlantic in a small boat with a guy who went crazy and tried to throw him overboard, from harrowing cliff climbing in Yosemite to getting lost in the jungles of Nicaragua, it was clear that Rob was using an entirely different set of criteria than mine to make life decisions.

By the time I found him, Rob had slowed down considerably and was making his living as a freelance ski journalist in and around the Sierra ski resorts. Even in this "calmer" profession, Rob was still taking risks of a different order of magnitude than I would ever consider. Among his projects was a piece that had him going out for a week of night maneuvers in the wilderness with the US Marine Mountain Corps and writing various profiles of "extreme" skiers, which required him to accompany these athletes to venues that could only be reached by helicopter or worse.

When I asked Rob about whether he thought about the danger and the choices he was making—including their Present Value implications—he shrugged and said that he simply followed the path that seems most interesting and didn't really think too much about the consequences. He said he sometimes wished he had made more rational decisions that could have led him to have a family and more financial security, but on balance he felt lucky to have had as many experiences and memories as he had. In the calculus of value, it was clear that Rob knew his mind and was making trade-offs that made sense for him. What he never did, and never felt he had to do, was to consider the future and incorporate Present Value into his decision-making.

And then, suddenly, everything changed.

It was 2008 and Rob was training for a trip to Antarctica where he was going to accompany some explorers and extreme skiers on their quest to find and ski some peaks that had never been skied before. But the training was harder than it should have been, and it became clear to Rob that something was wrong with his body. When he finally went to the doctor, he was given the devastating news that he had cancer of the appendix—a rare and extremely lethal form of the disease. He was told that his cancer was so deadly that patients like him typically survive less than six months, and his chance of living more than two years was essentially zero. Even grimmer was the fact that in order to have a chance of surviving that long, Rob would need to undergo not just aggressive chemotherapy, but multiple major surgeries.

For the first time in his life, Rob was faced with choices that *required* him to think in terms of Present Value. He knew what the next six months would entail, what the quality of his life would be like if he chose not to treat his cancer, and he knew exactly how much pain and suffering he would have to endure if he chose to fight the disease. What he didn't know was how long the treatment would keep him alive and what he was going to do with the extra time that he might be able to obtain—Rob's planning horizon was usually measured in weeks, and the idea of thinking that far in advance was truly a foreign concept—and whether in the next two years additional treatments might come along that could extend his life even further (in some ways, the most valuable aspect of the extra time). For almost fifty years, Rob had avoided doing so, but now he was going to have to consider the future, albeit a shorter one than most of us think we have.

Like every other challenge he had faced before, Rob threw himself into this one with clear eyes and courage. Very quickly he came to the conclusion that for him, life itself and the ability to engage with it was worth almost any price. After being assured that in between surgeries and chemo treatments, he would be relatively pain-free and mobile (at least until the treatments failed to be effective) he started to think concretely about what he wanted to accomplish in the time he might be able to purchase (steps 2 and 3). And it was a surprisingly long list. In addition to various projects that he was in the middle of, he decided he wanted to cover a major ski event in France and actually get to Antarctica. Interestingly, as he thought about how important those future experiences were compared to current costs (step 4), it was apparent that his personal rate of discount was essentially zero, an ironic result for someone who had lived his entire life in the present moment. So valuing those future experiences far more than the near-term pain, and hoping that buying extra time would allow technology to catch up with his disease (step 5), he jumped in to battle his cancer with every weapon he and his doctors could marshal.

One other—somewhat less surprising but equally idiosyncratic—aspect to the way Rob faced his dilemma was how little he considered the financial aspects of the decision. Having no wife or children who might eventually have to bear the financial burden of his illness, Rob had the luxury of ignoring the financial cost of his treatment without any legal ramifications. For him, it was a "no brainer." If the hospital or doctor was willing to perform the service, he accepted it. At one point I remember visiting him in his apartment and seeing a stack of over $100,000 worth of unpaid medical bills. Seeing the look on my face, he smiled and observed how crazy he thought it was that some people considered that stack more important than the value of the precious time that the treatments had provided him.

The final bittersweet irony of this last aspect is that Rob actually lived for two and a half years after his diagnosis, and once he passed the two-year mark (which his doctors had never seen before), he became a medical curiosity and the cost of all his medical treatments became free as the medical establishment decided that (on a Present Value basis) it was worth investing *their* resources in Rob so that they might be able to extend the lives of others with the same diagnosis.

It was a fitting final chapter to a life well lived by a remarkable individual who epitomized what it means to make the right choices by staying completely aware of his *own* desires and values.

Medical Tests and Lifestyle Choices

Rob's story is extreme, and his choices were particularly stark and short term, but millions of us have faced and will face serious decisions about our health and medical procedures that most of us are ill equipped to grapple with. Many of these choices have implications that extend far into the future, and so Present Value thinking can be an extremely useful tool in making them. Unhappily, most doctors don't think that way, and consequently the information and alternatives we are provided can sometimes prevent us from thinking about our choices in the most productive way.

For example, when my wife was pregnant, the doctors suggested, (as they do with any woman over age thirty-five), that she might want to undergo a somewhat risky and invasive test to check for various birth abnormalities.[51] Their rationale was that "at her age, the probability of the test causing a miscarriage is less than the probability of your child having Down's Syndrome."[52] To me, this completely missed the point. Certainly the likelihood of each of these devastating events is relevant, but conflating them into a "simple" comparison like this seriously distorts the nature of the decision.

First, and most obvious, the choice is not between a miscarriage and a Down's syndrome baby. The choice was between risking a miscarriage and *not knowing* whether or not our child was going to be normal. It's the value of that knowing (the probability of which was 100% if the test was taken) that needed to be compared to the risk of the procedure. Secondly, the two results themselves were not even comparable in "value." A miscarriage would happen immediately and would cause us one kind of pain and suffering while having a Down's Syndrome child would have an entirely different kind of "cost" that would extend over many years in the future. Maybe the assumption on the doctor's part was that faced with the prospect of a disabled child we would choose to terminate the pregnancy, but that to me seems extremely presumptuous on his part and even while those two events—a miscarriage and an abortion—would occur at approximately the same time, they are fundamentally different in nature. A pregnancy termination would abort a fetus *known* to be abnormal, while a miscarriage would end a pregnancy that had *over a 95% probability of producing a normal baby*. To me this is not just a practical difference but a moral one as well.

It should be obvious by now that the right way to think about the pregnancy test above is by using Present Value. At the end of the day, that is what my wife and I did. Hard as it was, we clarified our choice (take the test or not), imagined the possibilities, frightening as they were, and *correctly* used the probabilities we were given to weigh the present values of the consequences of each choice. We then nervously (and with full awareness of our choice) decided to take the test and to our delight had no problems with the test and found out that our son was going to be perfectly normal. When I think of the thousands of others facing this or similar questions without the tool of Present Value at their disposal, it makes me very sad and even more committed to spread the word about how poorly informed we often are about some of the literally life-and-death choices that we face.

Unfortunately, I believe that this sort of muddy thinking and misapplication of probability and statistics is not limited to acute treatment options. With the advancement of technology and medical research, more and more of our ongoing health maintenance decisions (e.g., diet and lifestyle) have become confusing with an army of experts proffering advice and statistics to get us to change our habits to extend or improve our life, but no guide to provide us a systematic way to sort through the information to make the right choices. I hope it is clear by now that Present Value thinking and the five steps entailed in the process can be extremely helpful in that regard.

Space does not allow me to go through the details of how a Present Value analysis can be useful in deciding on whether to go "gluten free," start an exercise regime, or stop (or start) drinking wine, but by now the recipe should be familiar. My advice is the same as that I have provided throughout. In particular, be very attentive to steps 3 and 4. The fact that there are statistics that bear on the efficacy of the regimen (diet, herbal, etc.) you are considering does *not* mean that the probabilities presented are "true" and, more important, that they are the right ones for you to factor in to the decision, particularly when the costs are immediate and the benefits are far in the future.

Whatever the choice is, as long as there are costs and benefits involved with some of those costs/benefits emerging both now and at different points in the future, you can use Present Value to help you make your decision. You don't have to translate the value of what you are considering into dollars. You don't even have to put any kind of specific number on it at all. All you have to do is weigh those costs and benefits by your own internal scale, determine their *relative* values, and then layer on your own personal rate of discount to complete the picture.

Chapter 12

PRESENT VALUE AND THE DISTANT FUTURE —PLANTING TREES AND LEAVING A LEGACY

About two years ago, my wife and I bought a small farm north of San Francisco. With eight acres and two (run-down) houses on the property, it was only an hour away from our jobs and therefore an ideal short-term weekend getaway, a long-term retirement home for us, and maybe—if we are lucky—a place where our son and his family might one day come and stay. I can't honestly say that I did a Present Value analysis when we bought the place. The simple fact was that we saw the property and just fell in love with it. But that being said, now that we own it, we are constantly having to make decisions that have Present Value at their core.

Most of those decisions are of a mundane, day-to-day type that we talked about in chapter 2 (e.g., whether to rewire one of the houses, put a new septic system in, and/or convert to solar energy), but more than a few are decisions whose future consequences extend beyond our lifetime. For example, the people who owned the property before us had a variety of animals. There were horse stables, chicken coops, and several fenced-in pastures for goats and sheep to graze. This is not our kind of farming, and so over the last several months we have been dismantling the infrastructure designed for livestock and thinking about what to put in its place.

Much of the property we want to keep clear and beautiful for walks and contemplation, but we also want the place to produce food, so we are now in the process of designing and planting an orchard, and here is where the Present Value considerations get very interesting. The variety of fruit and nut trees that could grow and flourish in this part of the country is quite large. Citrus, stone fruit, apples, pears, persimmon, pomegranates, avocados, olives, and a dozen kinds of nut trees are all possibilities, and each variety has its own particular personality and characteristics. In particular, each type of tree will take a certain number of years before it starts producing fruit and then have a productive lifespan that will vary considerably from tree to tree. Beyond that, each one will require a different level of care and have a different "risk profile" that will include not only the variability in year-by-year yield, but also the risk of early demise through disease or weather catastrophe. In short, with fifty trees to be planted, we have fifty different Present Value decisions to make.

It was also sobering to realize that at our age, the orchard we are planting will be around for decades after we are gone, and so the Present Value calculations we do need to take this into account. Unlike the time horizon we talked about earlier, we *do* care and place value on what the orchard will look like and produce after we are gone. It is a legacy that we will leave to our son and/or to those that may own the property in the future, and it has caused us to think hard about that distant future and make choices that go beyond those of chapter 11, where money doesn't matter, to those where we are not even the ones who will face their consequences. Counterintuitive as it may be, I believe that Present Value thinking is just as important here as in any of the other types of choices we have discussed previously.

Leaving a Legacy

Much of this book has been focused on becoming conscious of the "time horizon" that is inherent in every decision that is based on Present Value. And there is no time horizon starker than one's own death. None of us like to think about our eventual demise, but there are many decisions we make (or should make) whose consequences extend beyond our lifetime. The entire life insurance industry is built around the proposition that individuals should think about the next generation and what we will leave behind. As a result of our difficulty in thinking truly long term, they say that life insurance is "sold not bought," and in many ways that's true. If I hope to accomplish anything with this book it is to help readers take better control of many of the decisions in their lives and to "buy" rather than "be sold," particularly when it comes to those decisions with consequences far in the future.

Right now, I am not going to tell you how to buy life insurance, but I do want to talk about a kind of decision and an opportunity that I believe more of us as individuals should consider and those of us who work at not-for-profit organizations should be attentive to. It's the kind of decision where Present Value is front and center and where an individual can potentially impact the world in a positive way. It is also an area where a not-for-profit organization needs to consider Present Value very carefully. Specifically, I want to talk about the decisions we will all have to make eventually about where the assets we accumulate over our lifetimes will go when we are gone.

In 2001, my partner and I sold our little consulting firm to a big insurance brokerage firm, and I was given a relatively large lump sum of money. It was not so large as to radically change my life, but it was enough so that I needed to find a long-term investment for it and ideally do so in a way that would enable me to avoid paying a lot of up-front taxes. By now, it should be no surprise that I went through our 5-step process to evaluate the various alternatives I had with respect to using (or investing) the money. After going through the process, I decided to look for some kind of guaranteed lifetime annuity that would begin paying me when I retired. Unfortunately I was only forty-five years old, and far too young for an insurance company to be willing to make the kind of long-term investment guarantees that would be required to sell me such a product. As luck would have it, my old school heard about my windfall, and I got a call from Sam (the Planned Giving Officer) who, after hearing the details of my situation, presented me with the opportunity of obtaining a Charitable Gift Annuity (CGA) from the school.

The annuity I was offered was similar in structure to that of a traditional annuity purchased from an insurance company.[53] In this case, however, I would be able to combine my retirement planning objectives with the ability to benefit my alma mater. Specifically, I would make a large lump sum contribution to the school, and in return the school would promise to provide a guaranteed stream of payments to me that would begin when I turned sixty-five and continue for the rest of my life. The only difference between this and an annuity purchased from an insurance company was that my contribution would be considered a gift to the school because, upon my death any funds remaining after all annuity payments had been made would revert to the school's endowment. As a result, in addition to receiving the guaranteed lifetime income, I would *also* receive an immediate tax deduction for the Present Value of what the school expected to recover from my contribution (and all the investment income they were able to earn on the funds) after I died.

Essentially, obtaining the CGA was like buying an annuity from an insurance company except that instead of profiting the insurance company, I would be making a deferred gift to an organization that I cared about. Surprisingly, however, the terms of my annuity (guaranteed income beginning *twenty years* after the purchase) were better than I could get from any insurance company then in the market. This seemed too good to be true. While Sam was an attorney and clearly knowledgeable about the mechanics of how CGAs (as well as all the other more esoteric Planned Giving products) operated, he was not an actuary and seemed unaware of how financially attractive to me (and risky to the school) this arrangement was. After checking the numbers and the documents to make sure I wasn't missing anything, I signed up and purchased my CGA, feeling satisfied with my investment but just a little embarrassed (and concerned) by how grateful Sam seemed at the "extremely generous" gift to my alma mater.

The experience sent me scurrying to find out more about Planned Giving in general and the CGA market specifically. What I found was a world full of opportunity and risk that is operating, in my view, without adequate actuarial guidance. It turns out that when charities and other not-for-profit organizations (e.g., universities and hospitals) offer CGAs (as well as other "legacy" gift opportunities) to potential donors, IRS rules provide that such donors can get an immediate tax deduction for their deferred gifts. That is why I was able to get an immediate tax deduction for my purchase even though the school wouldn't get full access to my contribution until (hopefully) many years from now. But the flip side of this is that—theoretically at least—charities are supposed to structure these arrangements in such a way so that a large portion of the initial amount contributed reverts to the charity when the donor dies. In fact the American Council on Gift Annuities (ACGA) does provide CGA rate guidelines to charities,[54] but because the charities are often short on internal expertise, these guidelines are often misinterpreted or misapplied. You are *not* supposed to get an annuity that provides more retirement income from your alma mater than from a company like Prudential Life Insurance.

After this discovery, I started talking to my not-for-profit clients about their Planned Giving programs and attending Planned Giving conferences to hear what the professionals had to say about how these programs are structured and what issues are current. Everyone seemed unfailingly excited about the future of Planned Giving and most of the talk centered around "marketing" and how charities could all get their fair share of this growing and potentially enormous market. And enormous it is. The estimates I've seen suggest that when the Baby Boomers eventually die they will leave behind about *$41 trillion.*[55] To me, the question of where that money goes and how it is managed is one of the important Present Value questions facing society today. Clearly, insurance companies and the financial services industry in general have their eyes on this pot of money. But, in a perfect world, charities and other not-for-profit organizations that benefit society should get a lot of it as well. In fact, the system is designed for that to happen because of the tax breaks donors receive and people's inherent desire to benefit organizations that are trying to make the world a better place. Unfortunately, right now charities are losing the battle due to the public's lack of awareness of these Planned Giving opportunities and the fact that for-profit companies (like insurance companies) have an overwhelming advantage when it comes to resources and expertise, particularly in the area of product development and sales.

I spoke earlier about how Planned Giving represents great risk and opportunity for charities. The opportunities are easily understood and fairly well known to the executive directors and management of most large not-for-profits. Being able to grow their endowment by having donors contribute lump sums now in return for making payments in the future is a benefit that you don't have to be an actuary to appreciate, but even in the basic transfer of funds there are nuances that many organizations fail to pick up on. For example, because a CGA is a legally binding contract that a charity enters into, there are potentially better ways to structure a deferred gift by using what are known as Charitable Remainder Trusts (CRTs)[56] that essentially provide the same benefit (and more flexibility) to donors without the same legal restrictions inherent in a CGA. Beyond that, a direct bequest (i.e., writing the charity into your will) can provide a *Present Value* benefit to a charity that is often undervalued by the Planned Giving community.

As important as Planned Giving opportunities are for both individuals and the organizations that provide them, it is a shared responsibility between donor and charity to ensure a win-win result. The donor should be willing to take a modest reduction in the Present Value of their own retirement income in return for being able to direct some of his or her ultimate legacy to a worthy cause (thus maximizing the Present Value of the financial *plus* non-financial impact of their accumulated assets). At the same time, the charity needs to be able to provide the opportunity to do so with knowledge and attention to the financial risks inherent in CGAs and other Planned Giving vehicles.

There is a good reason why the deferred annuity I purchased was not available in the general market, and that is because the CGA I got contained *interest rate guarantees* that extended far beyond the duration of any existing corporate or government bond. This is important, because any organization that guarantees a future payment stream needs to find a way to invest the money received in a way to have reasonable assurance of being able to meet those guarantees. Insurance companies do this by setting up sophisticated bond portfolios whose income stream will match the annuity payment obligations they take on. From what I've seen among the charities and other nonprofits I've talked to, the most common investment approach taken is for the charity to simply invest the funds received in the same way as the rest of their endowment is invested. To me this is a very risky approach, as stock market crashes and/or significant reductions in interest rates can suddenly create situations where the charity will actually *lose* money on the CGAs they issue.

In addition to the investment/interest rate risk, there is longevity risk that charities take on when they issue CGAs that should not be underestimated. In addition to the fact that most donors who obtain CGAs are both financially secure (though often not rich) *and* healthy, there is "anti-selection" risk where individuals who, for one reason or another (perhaps based on family history), know they are more likely than most to live a long time are therefore more inclined than the general public to buy an annuity. By now, you should recognize these concerns as those associated with steps 2 and 3 of our Present Value process and therefore won't be surprised to learn that insurance companies and their actuaries are very attentive to this risk and build in significant margins to their pricing to accommodate it. Beyond that, there are other more technical aspects to managing the risks of a Planned Giving program (e.g., concentration of risk in large contracts and fiduciary risk) where actuarial advice could provide a great deal of value.

As more and more Baby Boomers retire and consider their options for providing themselves with income to live on and think about the legacy they want to leave behind, I see a great need and an opportunity for society to benefit, but all concerned need to keep the principles of Present Value and the 5-step process front and center in their thinking. An opportunity like this is unique in history. Charities and other "mission driven" organizations are well positioned to address society's most pressing needs (from healthcare to education, to poverty, deprivation, and beyond) while at the same time there is a whole generation of Baby Boomers who *want* to provide their support but are largely unaware of how Planned Giving can provide the means to do so.

To their credit, the nonprofit world has so far taken the "high road" and has not competed directly with the financial services industry, relying instead on speaking only to their donors' philanthropic motivations, though as noted they often seem unaware of the risks they are taking on. While I don't think it will ever be appropriate for charities to "compete" with insurance companies, my opinion is that as the stakes get higher, they will need to change their message to the coming generation of potential donors and obtain more help from the actuarial profession in all aspects of this field. That support will include setting payout rates on CGAs and CRTs as well as managing the underwriting risks and advising charities on investing their assets and hedging their liabilities. Actuaries could even be valuable in engaging with Congress and the IRS to protect the tax advantages that charitable contributions for CGAs and CRTs deservedly enjoy and may come under attack when the rest of the financial services industry realizes the extent to which Planned Gifts could eat into their future profits.

It's a battle well worth winning, Present Value is the weapon of choice, and all of us can join the fight.

Chapter 13

THE VALUE OF THE ACTUARIAL PERSPECTIVE AND "THE REST OF YOUR LIFE"

Throughout this book, I have talked about how individuals, organizations, and even society in general should be considering Present Value when facing important (and not so important) decisions. It may seem, at times, that I am suggesting a perspective that is in some way revolutionary or "brand new." In fact, actuaries have been using Present Value for more than a century, and the questions that they address with that perspective are both important and affect almost everyone. Space does not allow me to describe the efforts of the many actuaries who are using Present Value to make things better, but I don't want to end our discussion without talking about two actuaries who are making a real difference in people's lives—one who focuses on the decisions individuals make and one who consults with the organizations for whom millions of us work. While the 5-step process for using Present Value lies behind almost all of what we as actuaries do, in this chapter I want to focus on the results of that work and talk about the true power of Present Value to make the world a better place.

Planning for the Future—The Role of Present Value in Improving the World

> *"As senior actuaries you should be excited to be practicing at a time when the country, and the world, is facing the most serious Retirement Income crisis we've seen in our lifetimes. Your knowledge and skills are* exactly *what the world needs now."*

> Gene Wickes, FSA, EA, and Global Retirement
> Leader of Towers Watson to the firm's
> most senior actuaries

The first time I met Gene Wickes was during the telephone company consulting project I talked about in chapter 7. As you recall, my old firm, Godwins, had been hired by a consortium of about a dozen regional telephone companies (Pac Bell, Bell Atlantic, GTE, etc.) who were collaborating in an effort to get the FCC to let them raise the rates they were charging AT&T (who provided all the long distance service) to use their phone lines. Now, these telephone companies were, by themselves, big corporations employing tens of thousands of employees each, and collectively they represented well over 100,000 employees as well as billions of dollars in assets and liabilities. Each of the companies had sent three or four executives (VPs from HR, finance, and regulatory affairs as well as more than a few lawyers) to an initial meeting to represent their particular interest and to plan their strategy.

The meeting took place in a huge conference room in the plush Washington, DC, offices of the industry's main lobbying organization (the United States Telephone Association "USTA") and there were nearly fifty people gathered around the largest conference table I had ever seen.

As I walked into the room, at that point, a young and relatively inexperienced actuary who had (with lots of help) basically bluffed his way into this assignment, I was more than a little intimidated. There clearly was a lot at stake. Everyone around the table was counting on me and my firm to deliver the analysis that would enable the companies to convince the FCC of their rights to AT&T's money, and at that point I had no idea of not only what our analysis would show, but also how we would actually perform it. It was a scary moment.

The only comfort I thought I could rely on was that I would be the only actuary in the room and therefore would be able to discuss actuarial aspects of the project from a position of some authority. Only I wasn't. Sitting several seats down and across the table from me was Gene Wickes. Of the twelve telephone companies who had decided to bring their most important individuals to attend this meeting, only one decided to send their actuary. Every one of the companies had an actuarial firm responsible for their benefit programs (and sometimes more than one), and every one of the actuaries involved knew about the effort with the FCC, but only Gene was viewed as an important enough advisor to his client—US West, the telephone company in Colorado—to be sent to this meeting.

What was even more remarkable than Gene's presence as trusted consultant to the US West contingent was the fact that during the three-hour meeting on issues ranging from coordinated regulatory strategy to the assumptions and methods that we were going to use in our actuarial analysis, Gene never said a word. His silence told me two things about him that I would see manifested again and again in the years following. First, his relationship with his client was so good that US West was obviously willing to pay a great deal of money for him to simply observe and listen to the discussion, and second, he was so entirely focused on the group getting to the right answer that he was willing to put aside his ego and, unlike 99% of the consultants I know, not feel the need to voice his opinion when he felt that it would not contribute meaningfully to the objectives of the group as a whole.

In the twenty years after that first meeting, I came to know Gene very well as a colleague, a competitor, then as my manager, and finally as the global retirement leader of the firm where I currently work. In that time, my respect and admiration for him has continued to grow as I have watched him take on bigger and broader challenges each step of the way. To my mind, Gene epitomizes the way actuaries can use the power of Present Value and the actuarial perspective in general to help make the world a better place.

With a degree in math and economics from Brigham Young, Gene came to the profession with somewhat less formal mathematical training than many actuaries, but in all my years I have never seen an actuary who can absorb a technical piece of analysis as quickly and completely and, far more importantly, be able to hone in on the key results and communicate those results clearly and effectively in plain English to his clients and the public at large. As a devout Mormon, Gene also brings to his work an orientation that, while not exactly "mission driven," is based on a rock solid moral foundation, extraordinary integrity, and a belief that as actuaries we should be looking at all times to do the "right" thing and use our skills in a way that will help make the system better for all.

Gene has done many things in his career, has helped some of the largest companies in the world manage their retirement plans, and currently sets the direction and oversees the efforts of over 2000 actuaries at Towers Watson. Right now, he is focusing his efforts on bringing to bear the resources and expertise of our firm to address one of the biggest Present Value problems facing this country—and the developed world in general—today. Specifically, he is concerned with how to fix a global retirement system that is badly broken and threatens to cause enormous suffering and distress to millions of people who will, within the next few decades, be too old to work and yet not have enough to live on for the rest of their lives. Theoretically, in the United States (as well as most other countries), retirement income is supposed to be provided through a "three-legged stool" representing a combination of employer sponsored retirement plans, Social Security, and personal savings that an individual has set aside from his or her own funds. Unfortunately all three of these legs are falling short of their goal. The US

Social Security system is facing long-term massive deficits and will likely need to be cut back, employers have sharply curtailed their retirement plans, and individuals have not been able or willing to set aside enough of their current income to provide for their future needs.[57]

This is an extremely complicated problem with many aspects. Clearly, the health of the US Social Security system is a key piece of the puzzle, as well as the failure of individuals to save enough. Both of these problems have Present Value at their core. In the case of Social Security, the fact is that the US government has not paid sufficient attention to their own actuaries and the Present Value analyses they have been producing every year since the system was introduced. The problem of individuals and their behavior is something we will talk about shortly, but where Gene and his actuaries are focusing their efforts and are having a big impact is among company-sponsored retirement plans.

Over the last twenty years, companies' commitment to providing retirement benefits to their employees has declined significantly. Pension plans have been frozen and terminated and company contributions to 401(k) plans and other defined-contribution retirement plans have not made up the difference.[58] Part of this trend has been driven by companies taking advantage of the high personal rates of discounts that most people have. Many companies with some justification say that they are only trying to be "efficient" and get the most employee relations "bang" for their compensation "buck" and giving $1 of extra salary is more desirable to the average employee than putting an extra $2 into the pension plan. Essentially, they have used Present Value to create a "win-lose" situation with their employees. While this is arguably a case where Present Value has been misused and one that does society long term harm, it's hard to blame either the company or their employees for the result. Perhaps we should blame the actuary for not educating both parties as to how to use Present Value along the lines we have seen throughout this book.

One silver lining in the financial crisis of 2008–2009 is that in its aftermath many more people *do* realize how important step 2 of Present Value thinking is (imagining all the possible futures) and now have a better appreciation for the value of a guaranteed pension plan, but this dawning realization may have come too late.[59] As of 2010, over a third of all big companies who traditionally provided pension benefits to their employees had either frozen or terminated their plan and few of them, even with the greater awareness and desires of their workforce, have any appetite for reopening the plans.[60] Even worse, the new, largely high-tech companies that have grown explosively in the last few years employing greater and greater numbers of people, show very little interest in implementing new pension plans. The reason there has not been a resurgence in pension plans is related to the second cause for the exit of companies from the business of providing guaranteed pensions in the first place. Specifically, when companies do a Present Value analysis they come to the conclusion that the risk (investment, mortality, etc.) associated with providing a pension plan, at least the way it has historically been done, argues strongly for doing away with and/or staying away from sponsoring pension plans.

But Gene has helped companies look more deeply into those risks, do a better job imagining, and then evaluating the possible futures as well as identifying many of the non-financial aspects (both positive and negative) of providing (or not providing) pension benefits. Thus he and his colleagues have essentially used a much more sophisticated Present Value analysis as well as creativity in plan design to develop "win-win" ways of providing guaranteed lifetime retirement income promises (the essence of a pension plan) with only limited risk to the company's financial health.

Gene has led the charge by personally implementing new plan designs and financing strategies at dozens of companies and teaching the rest of the actuaries in the company how to do so with their clients. At the same time, Gene has been instrumental in spreading the word in the business community about the negative Present Value impact of *not* putting in a pension plan. Specifically, he notes time and again how the failure to provide employees a dignified and financially acceptable way of leaving the company will create a mass of "hidden pensioners" on the company payroll—large numbers of employees too old or sick to be productive, yet unable (due to a lack of a pension) to afford to retire. Without a way out, these hidden pensioners hang on to their jobs, bloating the payroll, reducing the overall productivity of the company, and stifling advancement opportunities for younger employees.

As Gene points out, there are risks in *every* approach—the key is for companies to understand those risks, determine which ones are most critical to their organization, and take steps to manage the ones that are unavoidable. He makes a very compelling case that for many—if not most—companies, those steps include providing a pension plan.

Only time will tell whether he will succeed. In the meantime, Steve Vernon is leading the charge in addressing the problem from another perspective— that of the vast number of individuals trying to figure out whether and how they will ever be able to retire and more generally how to map out their financial future.

Helping the Individual—How to Plan for the Rest of your Life

"How much money do you need and how can you make it last?"

Steve Vernon, FSA, President of Rest-of-Life
Communications, from his book *Money for Life*

And isn't that the key question that all of us ask ourselves all the time, not just as we are planning for retirement, but anytime we contemplate our financial situation? In this book, I have consciously avoided addressing the most common retirement and financial planning questions that we face. That may seem to be an odd decision for an actuary who has spent the last thirty-five years working with retirement plans, but the reason is quite simple. Those questions have already been written about eloquently and accessibly by someone in a way that provides all the guidance that anyone needs to make those important decisions, and I have very little to add to what Steve Vernon has said on the issue. The quote above is from one of Steve's books that is nominally about managing one's assets and income after retirement, but what he says can be viewed more generally and not just about retirement. As the name of his company suggests, Steve is focused on how we all manage "the rest of our lives": about what we need *today* to make sure we have enough *in the future.* In other words, he is talking about Present Value.

For over thirty years, Steve Vernon worked as a consulting actuary and for much of that time he and I worked for the same company, designing and redesigning pension plans as well as assisting our clients with the financial, compliance, and administrative challenges associated with those plans. During those years, Steve and I collaborated on numerous projects, and I always found him to be an extraordinarily quick study, uniquely creative in his thinking, but more than anything, a great communicator of complex topics to people with less expertise or technical knowledge than him. Steve is a gifted writer, and his books (he has written five) are remarkable in their clarity and flow. He makes actuarial concepts and retirement issues in general easy to understand and downright fun to read about.

I first became aware that Steve was heading in this direction when it was announced at a regional meeting of the senior actuaries that Steve was going to be working part time for several months in order to finish the book he was writing. This was the first time I had ever heard of an actuary writing a book for the general public. It seemed like a quixotic venture, and knowing Steve's creativity and ability to write well, I was very curious to see what would emerge.

His first book, *Don't Work Forever*,[61] laid out, in clear and simple terms, basic actuarial concepts and the notion of planning for retirement in a way that anyone could understand, and his second book (*Live Long and*

Prosper[62]) expanded on the concepts to lay out a map and a thoroughly practical approach that can be used by people in their forties and fifties (and even younger) to make important choices about the rest of their lives. It was the first book that I had ever read that applied actuarial principles to thinking about all the issues that face us as we age and consider our money, health, family, as well as all the things we want to accomplish before we die. Not only that, but as an actuary with no agenda and no "product" to sell, his book contained guidance that was both insightful and completely unbiased. I started recommending the book to any and all friends who came to me looking for financial planning advice or recommendations for a financial planner to consult.

It was clear to me that Steve had found his new calling and that it would not be long before he left the actuarial consulting world. So I was not at all surprised to hear that in 2006, at the ripe old age of 53, Steve decided to retire from Watson Wyatt and start up his own consulting firm with the thoroughly appropriate name, *Rest-of-Life Communications*. He had seen a desperate need for millions of people for clear and unbiased advice on what to do as they faced the frightening prospect of aging without the resources, knowledge, or plan to enter this next phase of life.

At one point, I asked Steve how he planned to make any money with his new venture, given that he was not going to take commissions or sell any investment products, and the people who (desperately) needed his help didn't have the money, the understanding, or the motivation to pay for his time. He told me that he had no expectation of directly making money on his advice (at least in the short term), that he thought that what he had to say was important, and that he hoped that somehow it was going to work out, either through companies doing the right thing by hiring him to talk to their employees or finding some other revenue source to subsidize his writing and speaking.

Anyone who Googles Steve will see that his faith in what he has to say has been rewarded. His five books on retirement planning[63] are selling well, he has a regular blog on CBS MoneyWatch, he is a sought-after lecturer, and most recently he has been hired by Stanford's Center on Longevity as a Consulting Research Scholar to continue thinking, creating, and writing about how we all can make the rest of our lives as long, healthy, and productive as possible.

To me, Steve Vernon epitomizes the importance of the actuarial perspective and the power of Present Value. While he never uses the term explicitly, the concept lurks behind all the great advice he provides on making those decisions that will inform and improve the "rest of your life," and I advise anyone who has enjoyed this book to pick up a copy of one of his.

A Final Word on How Present Value Can Make All the Difference

In 1994 I met a woman who changed my life. Visiting friends in Berkeley over winter break, I first set eyes on Tali at a Chinese restaurant on Christmas night. Dark, brilliantly creative, intense, deep, and frighteningly beautiful, I was immediately smitten, but with so many others at the table we had only the briefest opportunity to talk. It was several months before I was able to find my way back to Berkeley again, but when I did, during the summer of the following year, I engineered a reintroduction and got to know her a bit more.

Tali had come to San Francisco in 1989 from Israel, arriving just in time to experience a major earthquake that wrecked the neighborhood to which she had just moved six days earlier. Her life in Israel, as well, was as different from mine as could possibly be imagined. As a seven-year-old child in Jerusalem, she spent most of the Six-Day War hiding in a bomb shelter with her mother and two brothers while the battle for the city raged on above their heads while her father was in the Sinai Desert fighting the Egyptians. The fact that her father had spent his childhood in Egypt and was fighting against soldiers with whom he had grown up only made it harder for Tali to make sense of the chaos and irrationality that surrounded her.

By the time we met, Tali had just gotten a PhD in psychology to go along with her other graduate degrees in philosophy and art as well as a tour of duty in the army, several months in an Israeli military jail for refusing to carry a gun, and the better part of a year spent living on a kibbutz that produced decorative flowers for florists around the world and plastic wrapping for meat products found in supermarkets. Her perspective on the world in general and the future in particular was, to say the least, informed by a different literature and a different set of experiences than mine.

A woman like Tali had no shortage of suitors and the competition for her attention was fierce. Given her attitude toward the future (I would eventually learn that one of her favorites phrases is "why not now?") and her clear desire for a family, I knew I had only a small window of opportunity to make my case.

Almost immediately, I was put to the test as on our very first date she told me that with her almost-empty bank account and massive student loans she was worth "negative $100,000" and asked me whether that was going to be a problem. Knowing the pressure was on, I performed the fastest (and most important) Present Value calculation in my life. In addition to guessing that the Present Value of her future earnings as a psychologist was much more than the $100,000 she owed the bank, I imagined the possible futures and realized that the Present Value of the benefits of having a life with Tali was so large as to make the choice absolutely clear. Even then, however, I sensed that we spoke different languages, and she might not fully understand my reasoning, and so instead of explaining, I simply answered her with a straightforward, "Not in the least."

It was the best decision of my life and a Present Value calculation that I have never once had cause to regret.

At the end of the day, we all must live in the present and move into the future with as little fear and as much awareness as we can manage. We really have no choice. I often think about life as a hike on a trail in the mountains that we take in the middle of the night equipped only with our senses, what we can carry on our back, and perhaps a small flashlight that we can use to see a few feet in front of us.

Think about Present Value as that flashlight. Keep it close, use it often, and focus its beam where it can best illuminate the places where the trail is rough and the way forward is unclear. I can't promise that you'll never choose the wrong path, but if you shine it on the right spots, at least you'll know where you are headed and why.

Notes and References

Introduction

1. Eckhart Tolle, *The Power of Now* (New World Library, 1997).
2. Daniel Kahneman, *Thinking, Fast and Slow* (Penguin Books, 2011).
3. Shane Frederick, George Lowenstein, and Ted O'Donoghue, "Time Discounting and Time Preference: A Critical Review." *Journal of Economic Literature* Vol. XL (June 2002): 351–401.

Chapter 1

4. The most important of the many was Stephen G. Kellison, *The Theory of Interest* (R. D. Irwin, 1970).
5. All the details on what it takes to become an actuary can be found at the Society of Actuaries website (www.soa.org).

Chapter 2

6. Some readers have pointed out that I left out the fact that by buying a new refrigerator I was accelerating the point where I would need to buy *another* one (and another one after that). In other words I should have been calculating "the Present Value of all future refrigerator expenses." It turns out that, while true, this has a very minor impact on the analysis and doesn't change the result, especially when you consider that discount rates for the distant future (at least mine) are *higher* than 5%. This point also is true for the "air duct" example a little later on.
7. To my mind, Steve Vernon's books provide the best (and least biased) advice available on saving for and planning your retirement. He has written five of them and they can all be obtained (as well as other good information) at his website (www.restoflife.com).

Chapter 3

8. The world has changed somewhat, but even as of 2005 there were 31 credentialed actuaries disclosed in SEC proxy information as being in the

"top 5" of major insurance companies, and by the nature of the industry, high positions in Finance and other technical departments almost, of necessity have to be filled by actuaries. See for example (http://actuarialoutpost.com. actuarial_discussion_forum/showthread.php?t=12658).

9. For a succinct and well-presented history of the actuarial profession and its role in founding the insurance industry see http://www.actuaries .org.uk/research-and-resources/pages/actuarial-history-research and download Chris Lewin's 2007 seminar presentation on the subject.

Chapter 4

10. For those more quantitatively inclined, this note will give you more of the math behind Present Value. To derive the full general formula for a Present Value, let's first consider one of the most prevalent examples of present value that we see in the world, specifically the determination of our monthly payments when we buy a house and take out a mortgage.

Your Mortgage—Present Value When Payments are Certain

Most people understand that when you take out a 30-year mortgage, the higher the interest rate, the higher your monthly payments will be, but few people understand how those monthly payments are calculated. In fact calculating loan repayments is just the mirror image of a Present Value calculation, and an expansion of the above formula to consider *multiple* payments. If I take out a thirty-year mortgage on a $400,000 loan and the interest rate I get is 5%, my monthly payments will be about $2500 or $30,000 per year. If instead I look at it the other way and ask the question "what is the Present Value (using a 5% discount rate) of 30 years of monthly payments of $2500 per month?" The answer is $400,000. The way to see this is to think about each of those 360 monthly payments as separate present value calculations that when they are all added up sum to the amount of the loan. So even though the sum of all those payments equals $900,000 (i.e., 360 × $2500), the present value of the payments is exactly equal to the $400,000 you borrowed. Oversimplifying a little (by assuming each year's payments are paid in a lump sum at the end of the year) we can show this in numerical terms as follows:

$$\$30{,}000 \times (1/1.05) + \$30{,}000 \times (1/1.05)^2 + \ldots$$
$$+ \$30{,}000 \times (1/1.05)^{30} = \$400{,}000$$

Now consider what happens if mortgage rates go down to 4%. Everyone knows that when rates go down you should refinance to reduce your monthly payments, but the other way of looking at it is that because *discount rates* have gone down, the *Present Value* of all those future payments is now *more* than the $400,000 that you borrowed and you need to do something about it. You can check this for yourself by changing 1.05 to 1.04 in the above equation.

Life Insurance—Present Value When the Payment is Uncertain

The example of mortgage payments illustrates how to project the future and discount it back to the present to produce a Present Value when we are sure about what is going to be paid and when. But what if we are not? The simplest example of such a case is when you buy a single premium life insurance policy. Let's say you are thirty-five years old and you have a three-year old child. Suddenly you realize that even though you are planning your financial life in such a way that you will be able to save enough to put her through college, you need to do something about the risk that you might die before then. In particular let's say you expect that fifteen years from now you will have accumulated the $400,000 you think you will need to pay for four years of college, but if you die before then you won't have saved enough. Putting aside the complexities of exactly how much the actual shortfall would be and how much insurance you really need, let's say you decide to keep it simple and buy a life insurance policy that will pay your spouse $400,000 if you die some time in the next fifteen years and therefore be able to send your daughter to college. Let's further say that you just want to pay the insurance company one single premium that will cover you for the whole fifteen years. How much will such a policy cost and how does the insurance company determine it? To see how, we have to first understand that the amount of the premium should be the *Present Value* of all the future *possible* death benefit payments the insurance company *might* have to make if you were to die sometime in the next fifteen years. Now one approach to this might be to figure out the probability that you will die between the ages of thirty-five and fifty (about 5%) and apply that to the $400,000 to get the premium. But $20,000 (5% of $400,000) is too much because the $400,000 payment might not have to be made until fourteen years from now and we've already seen that $400,000 payable many years in the future is worth a lot less than $400,000 today. So what we need to do is to reflect *both* the uncertainty of the payment itself *and* the discount for the fact that *if* the payment is made, it will be made some time in the future. So much like we did with our mortgage payments, we need to evaluate the present value of each possible payment and then add them up. Specifically we first define the term $q(x)$, or simply qx, as the probability of someone age x dying before she reaches age $x + 1$. So q35 would be the probability of dying between ages thirty-five and thirty-six. Then assuming a 5% discount rate we calculate the premium as follows:

Premium = ($400,000 × q35) + ($400,000 × q36 x (1/1.05)) + ($400,000 × q37 × (1/1.05)²) + ... + ($400,000 × q49 × (1/1.05)¹⁴)

If you can understand the above equation, you understand present value. In fact the *basic equation* for present value in its general form can be expressed as:

$$\text{SUM } (t = 0 \text{ to } N) \text{ of } CF(t) \times P(t) \times (1/(1+i))^t \text{ where}$$

N = the number of years that is being considered in the calculation
CF(t) = the payment that is expected in year t (assuming it is made)

P(t) = the probability that the payment in year t is actually made
i = assumed interest/discount rate

and "SUM (t = 0 to N)" is usually written as: $\sum\limits_{t=0}^{N}$, so that the whole formula with this notation is: $\sum\limits_{t=0}^{N} \dfrac{P(t)CF(t)}{(1+i)^t}$

The above equation is the complete and general formula for calculating Present Value.

Chapter 5

11. Mark is not his real name. Throughout this book I have tried to be as faithful to history as possible by contacting the people I am writing about directly. In this case, my friend objected to his actual name being used, so, at his request I have changed his name and occupation but not the essential facts of the story.

Chapter 6

12. Kurt Vonnegut, *Slaughterhouse-Five* (Delacorte, 1969).

13. Fritz Leiber, *The Big Time* (Ace Book, Inc, 1961).

14. Isaac Asimov, *Foundation (The Foundation Series)* (Spectra [Revised edition], 1991).

15. James Gleick, *Chaos* (Penguin Books [Revised edition], 2008).

16. Robert Pirsig, *Zen and the Art of Motorcycle Maintenance* (Bantam Books [New Age edition], 1981) p. 255.

17. Ibid. pp. 28–32.

18. For a description of the match, see www.chessgames.com/perl/chess .pl?tid=54195

Chapter 7

19. See for example chapter 11 of Nassim N. Taleb's *Fooled by Randomness* (Random House [Trade Paperback Edition], 2005), in which the author discusses a myriad of ways where we fail to accurately assess the probability of events and describes, in some detail, the groundbreaking work that Kahneman and Tversky have done in this area.

20. According to www.baseball-reference.com, over his career, Pedro Martinez gave up only 760 walks, putting him a lowly 286th on the all time list, but he hit 141 batters putting him comfortably in the top thirty of all time. As far as I can tell, his ratio of .186 is by far the highest of anyone with more than 100 HBPs. Interestingly, Greg Maddux at .137 (137/999) is not too shabby, either, as he is

one of only a handful of other pitchers with both more than 100 HBP and less than 1000 BBs over his career.

21. See again the Chris Lewin presentation mentioned in note 9.

22. Among other things, David's most important work on the appropriate way of funding a pension plan ("Objectives and methods for funding defined benefit pension schemes," *Journal of the Institute of Actuaries,* September 1987: 155–225) was never, in my opinion given the credit it deserves, and to this day very few actuaries have heard of the DABM (Defined Accrued Benefit Method).

23. See en.wikipedia.org/wiki/Bell_System

24. See en.wikipedia.org/wiki/Econometric_model

25. Nassim N. Taleb, *Fooled by Randomness,* Random House (Trade Paperback Edition), 2005.

26. Ibid. pp. 113–115.

27. Ibid. pp. 116–131.

28. Ibid. pp. 126–127.

29. See en.wikipedia.org/wiki/General_equilibrium_theory

30. See FCC Record, Volume 07, No. 09, p. 2724, April 20–May 1, 1992.

31. Nassim N. Taleb, *The Black Swan* (Random House [Trade Paperback edition], 2010).

32. From 1/1/1982 to 1/1/2000 the S&P 500 rose from 122.55 to 1469.25, a return of almost 15%/year

33. Taleb, *Fooled by Randomness,* 113–115.

34. There were countless postmortems after the LTCM collapse. See for example: Philippe Jorion, "Risk Management Lessons from Long-Term Capital Management," *European Financial Management 6* (September 2000): 277–300.

Chapter 8

35. Peter Neuwirth, "The Time Value of Time." *Contingencies,* Vol. 9 No.1 January/ February 1997: 47–50.

36. Frederick, Shane, George Lowenstein, and Ted O'Donoghue, "Time Discounting and Time Preference: A Critical Review." *Journal of Economic Literature* 40: 351–401.

37. Their website is at disability-insurance-specialists.com

38. One measure of this slipperiness can be seen by the extremely strong correlation between economic downturns and the level of disability payments made. This is not just with respect to *applications* for disability benefits, as one would expect when people experience economic hardship and seek income from other sources, but it turns out that when times are tough, the actual *rates of disability* increase as well. See for example the Statement of Stephen Goss (Chief Actuary of the Social Security Administration) given before the House Committee on Ways and Means on March 14, 2013 (www.ssa.gov/legislation/ testimony_031413a.html).

Chapter 10

39. See en.wikipedia.org/wiki/Discounted_cash_flow

40. Nassim N. Taleb, *The Black Swan* (Random House [Trade Paperback edition], 2010).

41. Frederick, Shane, George Lowenstein, and Ted O'Donoghue, "Time Discounting and Time Preference: A Critical Review." *Journal of Economic Literature* 40: 351–401.

42. See, for example www.forbes.com/sites/joannmuller/2014/02/21/pensions-spared-worst-pain-in-detroit-recovery-plan/.

43. See, for example www.nytimes.com/2013/12/04/us/politics/illinois-legislature-approves-benefit-cuts-in-troubled-pension-system.html?_r=0.

44. See www.oregon.gov/pers/docs/earnings_crediting1946-2012.pdf

45. See www.oregonlive.com/politics/index.ssf/2012/11/oregon_pers_money_match_pensio.html for an excellent article by Ted Sickinger, which includes a general description of how the Plan works as well as the history of how the Money Match arose and what steps were taken to remedy the problems that were created.

46. See www.oregon.gov/pers/docs/earnings_crediting1946-2012.pdf and find the amounts credited on "Money Match" accounts under the column headed "Tier One – Credited %."

47. In 2000 the *average* PERS participant retiring with thirty years of service received 100% of his pre-retirement income. This can be seen on page 5 of "PERS by the Numbers" September 2012 available at www.oregon.gov/pers/docs/general_information/pers_by_the_numbers9-2012.pdf

48. Ibid. p. 17.

49. See for example Justin Falk, "Comparing Benefits and Total Compensation in the Federal Government and Private Sector" *Working Paper Series of the Congressional Budget Office*, Washington, DC, January 2012.

50. See page 3 of "PERS by the Numbers" described in note 47.

Chapter 11

51. The test was Chronic Villus Sampling (CVS) and you can read about it at americanpregnancy.org/prenataltesting/cvs.html. The 1% probability of miscarriage is mentioned.

52. The probabilities of having a child with Down syndrome at different ages are can be seen at www.marchofdimes.com/baby/down-syndrome.aspx

Chapter 12

53. See for example Steve Vernon, *Money for Life* (Rest-of-Life Communications, Oxnard, California, 2012), pp. 55–58.

54. This is explained in concept on the American Council for Gift Annuities website at www.acga-web.org/about-gift-annuities-top/the-philosophy-of-gift-annuity-agreements.

55. Robert B. Avery and Michael S. Rendall, "Estimating the Size and Distribution of Baby Boomers' Prospective Inheritances," *American Statistical Association, Proceedings of the Social Statistics Section*, 1993. pp.11–19.

56. Charitable Remainder Trusts are explained in detail on the Planned Giving Design Center's website at www.pgdc.com/pgdc/charitable-remainder-trusts.

Chapter 13

57. One of the best discussions of how the retirement crisis arose can be found in Sylvester Scheiber, *The Predictable Surprise* (Oxford University Press, New York, 2012).

58. There is a wealth of data on this point available on the Towers Watson website (www.towerswatson.com).

59. "More U.S. Workers Willing to Trade Pay for Extra Security and Richer Retirement Benefits, Towers Watson Survey Finds," from www.towerswatson.com, February 27, 2012.

60. The fact that the predominant retirement program at most companies is now defined contribution and how those plans are managed is discussed in "The Defined Contribution Plans of *Fortune* 100 Companies" from www.towerswatson.com, February 2011.

61. Steve Vernon, *Don't Work Forever* (Wiley, 1995).

62. Steve Vernon, *Live Long and Prosper* (Wiley, 2004).

63. In addition to the two above, Steve's other books include *The Quest* (Rest-of-Life Communications, 2007), *Money for Life* (Rest-of-Life Communications, 2012), and *Recession-Proof Your Retirement Years* (Rest-of-Life Communications, Fourth Edition, 2014).

Acknowledgments

I like the term *acknowledgments* because it encompasses so much more than just saying "thank you" to a lot of people who helped me write this book. In fact, while I am filled with gratitude for the many who helped me in such a variety of ways, I also want to give credit, appreciation, and acknowledgment to how difficult the process has been on some of those who are closest to me.

First, foremost, and above all is my wife Tali. When I met Tali, I was a very narrowly focused career-oriented actuary with a very specific plan and a singular path to follow. She opened my mind and opened my heart to all the wonderful possibilities that the future could embrace. More than anyone, she is the one who taught me to imagine the future, to look within myself for what I most value and to have the faith that others might want to hear what I have to say. Throughout this process she has been a rock I could lean on, a confidante to share my doubts with, and a compass to help guide me toward my destination.

While Tali was my inspiration, there were many others without whom this book would not exist. Most important of those is Steve Piersanti and his entire Berrett-Koehler team including my good friend Maria Jesus Aguilo, who felt my book belonged at BK and introduced me to Steve. The encouragement and support that Berrett-Koehler provided me as a first time author was simply incredible, and many times I wondered why such a company would risk spending so much time and attention on an "untested" product like myself. I only hope I can prove their investment was worthwhile and that their "Present Value" analysis was correct.

Many of my closest friends and family helped me write this book. Among the earliest and most important was Jerry Sontag, a friend who believed in me from the beginning and whose offer to publish the book himself, gave me the confidence to keep going whenever I had doubts about the worthiness of the project or my ability to complete it.

My parents Lee and Sydney Neuwirth, my son Adam, my sister Bebe Neuwirth, and her husband Chris Calkins have been steadfast in their support, love, and encouragement from before the beginning. More than just cheerleaders, they provided real and tangible help at many key points along the way.

I want to express special gratitude to my friend and former partner James Kenney who read every word of almost every draft from the perspective of an actuary, a friend, a business coach, and a prospective reader. Other close friends and colleagues who read drafts and provided both substantive and moral support included Henry Hecht, Rachel Durling, Gail Kurtz, Joel Ben-Izzy, Lucy Kaplan, Richard Ross, Eric Baum, Lorelei Sontag, Barry Sacks, and Alon Shalev.

In addition to James Kenney, I want to thank two other actuaries, Derek Cushman and Alan Glickstein, who provided a close reading of my work to make sure I wasn't misrepresenting the profession or making any technical mistakes.

I am also indebted to Steve Vernon, whose five great books showed me that actuaries can be writers, too, and who was incredibly generous with his time and advice on how to actually turn my ramblings into a coherent and potentially useful book.

To those who appear in the book—Mordecai Schwartz, Elise Pelke, Bob Walter, David McLeish, Andy Abel, Tad Verney, Bill Bossi, Charlie DeWeese, Gene Wickes, and Steve Vernon—I want to say thank you for allowing me to tell your stories. Not all of you were my teachers, but I learned something important about Present Value from each and every one of you.

Sadly, I can no longer ask Rob Frohlich for permission to tell his story. However, to his sister Margaret Pearcy I want to express gratitude for letting me share some of my memories of your remarkable brother.

I am also grateful to my employer, Towers Watson, for trusting that I would come up with something worthwhile as I was writing, and then throwing their support behind the project (particularly the senior leadership of the retirement practice as well as David Popper, Torry Dell, and Kathy Kibbe). I truly believe that there is no better firm for an actuary to work at than Towers Watson.

Finally I want to acknowledge the actuarial profession itself. For thirty-five years I have had the pleasure to work in a field where integrity, insight, mutual respect, and thoughtfulness are the norm. I feel proud to be an actuary, and that, more than anything is why you are reading these words today.

Index

About the Author

Peter Neuwirth has been an actuary for over thirty-five years, and after decades of having been asked too many times the question "What is an actuary exactly?" he has decided to go beyond answering that question to answer another—"How does an actuary think and why does it matter?"

Peter began his career after graduating from Harvard College in 1979 with a degree in mathematics and linguistics. After spending his first two years at Connecticut General Life Insurance (now CIGNA), he spent the next thirty-three in the consulting world, holding significant leadership positions at a variety of firms around the country, including most of the major consulting firms (Aon, Hewitt Associates, Watson Wyatt, Towers Perrin, and now Towers Watson) as well as spending five years as chief actuary at a regional benefits consulting firm (Godwins), seven years running a small actuarial firm (Coates Kenney), and one year in a large accounting firm (Price Waterhouse). He is currently a senior consultant at Towers Watson, serving as one of the firm's thought leaders and national experts in the area of financing nonqualified executive retirement plans.

Peter has consulted with dozens of the largest corporations in the world and worked closely with many

European based multinational corporations during the crash of 2008–2009, getting the unique opportunity to view the unfolding of the global financial crisis from the perspective of an American actuary doing business in Europe. This experience among many others in his career has provided him with a deep practical understanding of three of the fundamental concepts (time, risk, money) that shape our world. Many of those insights are shared in this book.

While this is his first book, Peter's work is well known in actuarial circles. He is a frequent speaker at professional conferences and has been quoted in both the mainstream and industry press on actuarial matters. He is a Fellow of the Society of Actuaries, an Enrolled Actuary under ERISA, a Member of the American Academy of Actuaries, and a Fellow of the Conference of Consulting Actuaries.

With a reputation among his peers as being a creative, knowledgeable, and experienced actuary with a penchant for both problem solving and thinking "outside of the box," Peter is also a storyteller who believes that the story of the actuarial perspective is one that needs to be told.

Pete lives in Berkeley, California, with his wife and son. You can visit his website at www.peterneuwirth.com.

About Towers Watson

Towers Watson is a leading global professional services company that helps organizations improve performance through effective people, risk, and financial management. With 15,000 associates around the world, we offer consulting, technology, and solutions in the areas of benefits, talent management, rewards, and risk and capital management. Learn more at www.towerswatson.com.

Berrett–Koehler
Publishers

Berrett-Koehler is an independent publisher dedicated to an ambitious mission: *connecting people and ideas to create a world that works for all.*

We believe that to truly create a better world, action is needed at all levels—individual, organizational, and societal. At the individual level, our publications help people align their lives with their values and with their aspirations for a better world. At the organizational level, our publications promote progressive leadership and management practices, socially responsible approaches to business, and humane and effective organizations. At the societal level, our publications advance social and economic justice, shared prosperity, sustainability, and new solutions to national and global issues.

A major theme of our publications is "Opening Up New Space." Berrett-Koehler titles challenge conventional thinking, introduce new ideas, and foster positive change. Their common quest is changing the underlying beliefs, mindsets, institutions, and structures that keep generating the same cycles of problems, no matter who our leaders are or what improvement programs we adopt.

We strive to practice what we preach—to operate our publishing company in line with the ideas in our books. At the core of our approach is stewardship, which we define as a deep sense of responsibility to administer the company for the benefit of all of our "stakeholder" groups: authors, customers, employees, investors, service providers, and the communities and environment around us.

We are grateful to the thousands of readers, authors, and other friends of the company who consider themselves to be part of the "BK Community." We hope that you, too, will join us in our mission.

A BK Life Book

This book is part of our BK Life series. BK Life books change people's lives. They help individuals improve their lives in ways that are beneficial for the families, organizations, communities, nations, and world in which they live and work. To find out more, visit **www.bk-life.com**.

Berrett–Koehler
Publishers

Connecting people and ideas
to create a world that works for all

Dear Reader,

Thank you for picking up this book and joining our worldwide community of Berrett-Koehler readers. We share ideas that bring positive change into people's lives, organizations, and society.

To welcome you, we'd like to offer you a free e-book. You can pick from among twelve of our bestselling books by entering the promotional code **BKP92E** here: http://www.bkconnection.com/welcome.

When you claim your free e-book, we'll also send you a copy of our e-newsletter, the *BK Communiqué*. Although you're free to unsubscribe, there are many benefits to sticking around. In every issue of our newsletter you'll find

- A free e-book
- Tips from famous authors
- Discounts on spotlight titles
- Hilarious insider publishing news
- A chance to win a prize for answering a riddle

Best of all, our readers tell us, "Your newsletter is the only one I actually read." So claim your gift today, and please stay in touch!

Sincerely,

Charlotte Ashlock
Steward of the BK Website

Questions? Comments? Contact me at bkcommunity@bkpub.com.